More Smart Marketing

More Smart Marketing

52 *More* Brilliant Tips and Techniques to
Boost Your Profits & Expand Your Business

Jeff Slutsky

Marc Slutsky

STREET FIGHTER

STREET FIGHTER

More Smart Marketing
Cover design by Jeff Slutsky

First published as a series of articles in a syndicated column for The Knight-Ridder News Service in 2001-2006.

To order this title on line, log on to: www.createspace.com/4403184
ISBN-13:978-0615869544 (Street Fighter Press)
ISBN-10:0615869548

Contents

Other Books by Jeff Slutsky

- *Smart Marketing* (coauthored with Marc Slutsky)
- *Smart Selling* (coauthored with Marc Slutsky
- *Street Fighter Marketing* (with Marc Slutsky)
- *How to Get Clients* (with Marc Slutsky)
- *Street Fighter Marketing Solutions*
- *The Toastmaster's Guide to Successful Public Speaking* (coauthored with Michael Aun)
- *From the Big Screen to the Real World* (coauthored with Larry Winget)
- *No B.S. Grassroots Marketing* (coauthored with Dan Kennedy)
- *Street Smart Tele-Selling*
- *Streetfighting: Low cost advertising for your business* (coauthored with Woody Woodruff)
- Street Smart Marketing

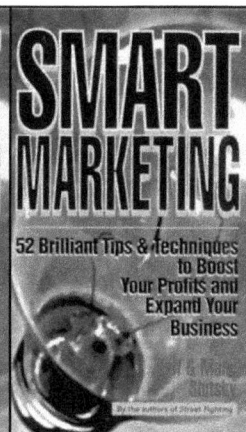

www.streetfightermarketing.com
800slutsky@gmail.com

Dedication

This book is dedicated to Howard and Sonia Eichenwald. The best in-laws I could ever ask for. Seriously!

Introduction

More Smart Marketing is the second of a series of books, based on our Knight-Ridder News Service weekly column, BizSmart. These articles provide you with clever, shrewd and smart tips, hints and anecdotes that allow you to get more out of your business with less money. You'll discover the inside tricks and techniques from some of the most successful and creative people from around the world. It's presented in a vignette-like format that is sure to keep you interested, motivated, and mesmerized.

More Smart Marketing provides 50 more short chapters, one for each week of the year. The topics are in all areas of marketing, advertising, promotion, customer service, management, operations, finance and sales and are applicable to many types of business. The goal of this book is to provide an understanding of how to run a more profitable business. We suggest that each week you read one chapter to your specific business. Your success will come from the adaptation of these ideas to your needs and unique opportunities.

A "Smart Marketing Action Plan" is provided at the end of most of the chapters to help you convert the ideas into action. Use these 50 chapters as "thought starters." We want you to get thinking more creatively about your business. But it is your job to take the ideas to the next level. Modify. Adapt. Improve. Make them work for you.

We have conducted many consulting and training programs throughout the country for a variety of businesses, large and small, including McDonald's, Goodyear, Marriott, Chevron, Molson, Subway, Pizza Hut, Sony, Firestone, USPS, and the US Army.

Jeff Slutsky
& Marc Slutsky

For information about keynote speaking, seminars, books and consulting projects, contact Jeff Slutsky at 800slutsky@gmail.com. 800-758-8759 (800-SLUTSKY) web: streetfightermarketing.com.

Chapter 1

Using Special Recognition in the Sales Process

You can increase your closing ratio and your average sale by using awards your company has won in the sales process, according to Rayad Moore, President of the Consumers' Choice Award of Indianapolis, Indiana. Mr. Moore suggests that using such recognition only in the marketing and advertising ignores the huge competitive advantages you have earned by winning the various awards that are presented on the local level.

Building Trust. One of the biggest challenges that a sales person must overcome is gaining the trust of the prospect. Most prospects approach any kind of buying experience with caution. This makes trust a key factor in determining where a prospect will end up buying. This applies for those people shopping around more anything for a car to a funeral.

Early in the sales process, you should be asking many questions and listening very carefully to uncover what the major concerns and desires are of the prospect. By asking more questions, you can get the prospect to tell you many of his or her fears. Once that information is out in the open you can deal with it. Then you can probe to find out how important it is for that prospect to feel "comfortable" about buying from a given business. Try to discover how much that trust is going to play into the final selling decision. Don't assume anything here. This information must come from the prospect.

Once the prospect tells you, in his or her own words, trust will be a major element in the buying decision, then you can start to use the awards and honors you've received to reinforce your business' trustworthiness. For example, a car sales person may know that a given prospect is shopping several dealerships for the same basic car, looking for the best deal. But what is the best deal? Is it simply the lowest price or is it a low price coupled with top quality service? Once the prospect agrees that what is really wanted is a good price combined with a quality product and good service, then the focus is on "value." The award then is brought into the sales presentation to reinforce your claim that you provide the best value.

As in any sale, you must introduce the reinforcing elements at the right time to get the impact you want from your prospect. Don't rush it and don't volunteer the information until your prospect as agreed that "value" not just price, is what he or she really wants.

The Up-Sell. Another way to use an award happens when helping a buying customer understand the value of a more expensive package. Up-selling or suggestive selling is a critical part of the sales process and just as critical to the overall satisfaction of the customer. Though there may be price resistance when you offer a higher price item, service or add-on, oftentimes the customer will be much happier getting the higher quality version. The award can be used to reinforce that you're offering the add-on as a way to provide the customer that increased value.

Smart Marketing Action Plan:

- Once your company wins an award, incorporate it into the sales process.

- Help the customer to learn the difference between price and value.
- Use the award as a means to build trust with your prospect.
- Work the award into up-selling the customer.
- Only mention the award at the appropriate time in the sales process.

Chapter 2

Gift Certificate Practices That Turn Off Customers

Recently, I went to buy a gift certificate for my son's basketball coach. All the parents chipped in so we could present the coach with a $100 gift certificate to show our appreciation. One of our favorite places to buy gift certificates in Columbus is at Easton Town Center, a huge mall and shopping center with just about every regional and national retail store represented. The Easton gift certificates are good at most Easton retail stores, so it has always been a very appreciated gift which could be used to buy just about anything you can imagine. We've been buying these coveted certificates ever since the center opened.

On this trip we were disappointed. Easton had just started charging a $1.00 fee to issue the gift certificates. On my $100 certificate it really didn't make much difference but ahead of us in line was a woman who had just ordered a dozen $25 ones. When she was charged a $12 handling fee, she was very angry. I asked the attendant why they changed the policy and was informed that they wanted to recoup their cost in issuing the certificates.

With this change, the advantage to the customer is lost. Prior to instituting this $1.00 service fee, you could give a dollar amount of value which could be used like cash at several hundred different up-scale stores. Now you had to pay for the privilege. At this point we started giving checks for gifts instead of the Easton certificates.

Easton may have a very good reason for this new policy from a cost standpoint, however it now is a negative to their customers. If the goal is to get people to buy the certificates so that their merchants would receive the benefits of extra sales, then they have lost that edge. They're obviously not thinking about this from the customer's perspective.

Another negative event with gift certificates happened several years earlier. I had purchased a gift certificate at a major salon and day spa chain in Columbus. These were always cherished gifts. However, I found that the intended recipient preferred another gift so I thought it would be no big deal to get the name on the certificate changed to someone else. When I requested them to reissue the certificate they wanted to charge me a fee to do so and made it very difficult. They finally did. Yet, that experience was such a hassle that I have never purchased gift certificates from that company again. Though, my business may have only represented $200 a year, it's an approach that is not customer-friendly and therefore costs them business.

On a positive note, there is a local restaurant chain that offers a special deal around the holidays. If you buy $100 of gift certificates, you get a $25 bonus certificate for yourself. The $100 worth are treated just like cash. The $25 promotional ones have some restrictions. That doesn't bother us since we understand the rules from the beginning, plus it's an extra bonus on top of the value of the certificates.

SMART MARKETING ACTION PLAN:

For an effective gift certificate program:

- Treat your gift certificates like cash.
- Don't charge a service fee if you want customers to buy them regularly.
- Consider a bonus certificate promotion to increase sales.
- Make buying your certificates easy and painless.
- Reusable gift cards are more flexible than paper certificates.

Chapter 3

Off Shore Outsourcing Makes For Bad Customer Service

I found a charge on my American Express bill that I didn't recognize. I called the customer service 800 number on the bill, hoping to fix the problem. After punching, what seemed to be a billion or so numbers as requested, I was finally transferred to a real live person. The only problem was that I could barely understand a word this person was saying. She spoke in a very thick accent that I guessed was half way around the world. I had to have her repeat everything two or three times before I could finally understand what she was saying. Finally, out of frustration, I told her I would call back.

I immediately replaced the call. I punched in the billion or so numbers. Again, I'm greeted by someone with a very thick accent. This time a man was on the other end but he could have been the other person's uncle. Finally, after my third attempt, I found someone who could speak clearly enough that I could begin to get my problem resolved.

Of course Amex was outsourcing their customer service to an overseas company. I'm sure this practice saves them a lot of money. However, if you look at this practice from the customer's point of view, it actually may end up costing them a lot more. From my personal experience, I know that if I'm required to call their customer service once more and have any difficulty communicating in English, I'll simply cancel my card and start using one of my other ones instead.

When I was sharing this experience with an independent computer consultant, Kansas City based Howard Eichenwald; he warned of another problem with offshore outsourcing: Privacy. When an offshore company is privy to your sensitive information (i.e., your account numbers, your PIN numbers, your social security number, etc.) both the consumers and the business are at great risk of having that information end up in the wrong hands. You have to ask yourself what are the privacy laws of the country that now has access to sensitive financial or health data of the consumer. Also, what legal course of action does a corporation have as remedy should internal corporate information be disclosed to a competitor? Plus, identify theft can be a PR nightmare for a company.

Eichenwald, who has seen his industry lose much of their jobs to "Offshoring," suggests yet another negative effect on your business. This practice is sending jobs overseas and hurts the overall and local economy. People working in other countries do not pay taxes in the US. They also do not spend their salaries here in the US. The American workers they displace have less disposable income to spend in their local areas perhaps decreasing sales of products for the company that is trying to save some money by Offshoring. While some business may feel that it's not their problem, consider this: Sending jobs overseas has become a major issue. It's receiving a great deal of press. Lou Dobbs on CNN has a running feature focused exclusively on this. As a business, you are at risk of offending many of your customers. It only takes one unhappy customer to make waves with the press and your customers. You have to ask yourself if the savings is worth the risk. Even Jay Leno drew attention to this practice when he quipped, "The President was touting his economic record in Ohio last week, a state that's lost 225,000 jobs. If he really wants to tout his record, let him do it somewhere where jobs have actually been created — like India or Thailand or China."

SMART MARKETING ACTION PLAN:

- To stop the offshore outsourcing trend:

- When you deal with a department ask them <u>where</u> they are located.

- Write to company officials and let them know about your problems in dealing with their customer service representatives or that you do not approve of their offshoring jobs. Let them know that you are considering taking your business elsewhere because they offshore.

- Make your concerns known to your legislators.

- Send a copy of this article to company officials. Tell them I'm working on a follow up article on how "Offshoring" is bad for customer service and I want to use them as an example of what not to do.

Chapter 4

It's a Question of the Right Question

Some times a single word can make all the difference in business. In every transaction with customers and clients, you want to choose your words carefully. Often times the words that are used become so automatic, you may not stop to think if they are having an adverse effect on your business.

Case in point: I was in Eugene, Oregon consulting a restaurant client. I noticed that in several of their locations customers would go to the counter and order their meal and a drink. The counter person would respond with "what size?" In most cases the customer would say "medium." I then suggested that instead of asking "what size" they should ask "large?" That one word difference increases the number of large drinks sold. As you can imagine, there's a significant amount of increased profit on a high margin item like a fountain drink. When you consider how many drinks they sell over the course of a year, that restaurant increases it profits without adding one cent of extra marketing investment.

You could use the same approach when "up selling" or "suggest selling" an extra item. Almost everyone is familiar with the "would you like fries with that?" up sell approach. It can be very successful in selling more fries. But, since it's a question that requires either a "yes" or a "no" you could perhaps get a little better response by tweaking it slightly. "Which size fries would you like with that?" gives the customer several choices of "yes" responses to your offer.

On the other end of the spectrum are the words that are added that distract from the experience. For example, my wife and I want to an upscale restaurant. When greeted by the hostess, she asked, "*just* two of you tonight?" By adding the word "just" to her greeting, it made it sound like two wasn't a big enough party to be of interest. Keep in mind that she was very friendly and there was nothing in her attitude that was negative, yet when she added "just" to her greeting it took away from the experience. Instead, she could have simply said "two of you this evening?" which would have been more positive.

Servers ask the same useless questions. At the end of the meal they usually ask something like, "was everything okay?" Most people don't want to make waves so they'll answer with a perfunctory "yes" even if there was a problem. Now the server doesn't know the real story and therefore can't make it right. The customers leaves and never returns and when asked by friends, gives a less then positive report on the place. Conversely, if the server went to the extra effort of a more probing question like, "What else can we do that would have made your visit better?" That is likely to generate are more honest response, which gives you the type of feedback that helps to improve your customer service.

SMART MARKETING ACTION PLAN:

- Review the words and phrases you use when greeting customers.
- Look for responses that suggest the desirable end result.
- Give choices between two positives instead of all or nothing.
- Identify possible greetings that inadvertently convey a negative message.
- Encourage honest feedback from customers.

Chapter 5

Take Care Of Your Customers Now Or Someone Else Will

I go online to place an order for a case of double DVD cases. I've purchased this item many times from this one line vendor as well as CD jewel cases and quad-CD jewel cases. These items are used for the packaging of our various audio and video programs which were converted to the CD format last year. The problem is, this time I don't see the double DVD cases available. I then call the company direct to find out that they no longer carry the type of cases I use. They only carry the deluxe, more expensive version which cost quite a bit more than what we were paying. I was told by the company that the manufacturer discontinued this model. Of course this is upsetting because I have orders to fill and all my packaging inserts were designed around this particular case.

Out of desperation I did a search on Ebay. Eureka! I found several Ebay vendors who carried the same double DVD cases I needed. Now, I can continue to create my two CD sets. Since I'm still a little peeved at my original vendor, I also search Ebay for the other two types of CD jewel cases I use. Sure enough, there are several other vendors who carry exactly what I use. Plus, the prices for these items are about half of what I was paying before. I chose vendors that have at least a 99% positive rating from past buyers and I place my bids online. Once I win the auction (or use the "buy it now" function to bypass the auction process) I then pay electronically with Paypal. Three days later my orders arrive.

There are a couple of valuable lessons here:

1. From a business buyers' perspective, you should always be looking at other vendors, even if you're happy with your current one. That doesn't mean you should switch right away if you find someone who will sell to you for a few pennies less. But, if your current vendor should, for any reason, not be able to deliver what you need, it's good to have a back up.

2. Also, by shopping around it lets you know that you are still paying a reasonable price for your products or services. If your current vendors are getting complacent in your relationship, they may be charging you too much. It's okay to pay a little more if you know that vendor will service your account as needed. But to pay significantly more when all things appear to be the same is not smart business.

3. You an also use the information you find by shopping around as leverage with your current vendor. Price, service level and other elements can be negotiated if you know what others are offering. For example, if other vendors are offering free shipping and the purchase prices are the same, you would want to bring that to your current vendor's attention.

4. From a sellers' perspective consider this: If you drop a certain product or service it may have negative repercussions that you may not have anticipated. In my experience, the discontinued item caused me to look for another vendor. In that process, I found several vendors who offered better prices on all the different items I originally bought from the first vendor. Now that vendor has lost all of my business.

SMART MARKETING ACTION PLAN:

- Think carefully before dropping a product or service from your offerings.

- Comparison shop your current vendors to insure your prices are fair.
- Comparison shop to have a back up vendor just in case.
- Always look at what you offer from your customer's perspective.
- Explore new technologies to replace some you currently offer. We also offer our audio and video programs in both CD/DVD formats and MP3/MP4 downloads. The downloadable version not only is more profitable but a service the clients often prefer.

Chapter 6

Silent Auction Domination

A silent auction is a very popular and productive fund raising event for many organizations. Not only is it a good idea to support worthy causes by donating your products or services, but if you do it right, you can get great exposure. Of course, the big advantage of participating in a silent auction is that you're not donating hard dollars, but your product cost dollars.

Keep in mind that many of your potential customers attend these events, so you want to look for ways to get the most out of your efforts.

Up The Ante

Most businesses generally donate one or two items. However, some of the most popular offerings are those that provide a much higher total value. A few examples of this is the salon that donated one facial a week for a year. That created an item with a retail value of well over $3300, which created a great deal of interest. A local pizza restaurant did a similar thing by offering a large pizza a week for a year. Depending on the type of business you're in, you can really build value by packaging a number of your items into a weekly or monthly item for a year. This would also work easily with things including video rentals, car washes, food items, and so on.

Present Your Best

Many businesses offer items that are left in inventory or no longer popular. While on the surface it may make sense to unload this inventory for worthy cause. From a marketing point of view, you're not getting your bang for the buck. Consider, instead, offering your most popular items. Remember, many people will be exposed to your business name and what you do at these events. You want to make sure the participants associate you and your business with the products and services you want them to buy.

Not So Silent

Once you commit to offer a collection of product and services that have a significant retail value, leverage your donation by negotiating with the emcee to give you so many live mentions during the event. This was done by a jewelry store who donated a $1000 necklace. As part of the arrangement, the event agreed to mention the company and offering 10 times from the microphone and direct people over to his display.

Print The Program

In some smaller events, they may not have a program. If they do, it may not contain advertising. Offer to print their program for them, listing all the items, in exchange for your ad on the back cover. This would be a doubly perfect approach for a printer.

Ticket To Event

If the organization sells tickets to their silent auction, you can offer to print their tickets for them. Furthermore, to help them sell tickets, you suggest putting an on the back of the ticket that creates additional value. If tickets cost $25, you could offer $25 off the purchase of $100 or more at your business. It gives the impression that each person who buys a ticket gets their money back. Plus, you now have created an impression with everyone who attends the event, even before it happens.

Donate The Coffee

Most of these events will offer some kind of beverages or appetizers. If you donate those, you can have a sign at registration or near the food with your company name and logo. It could also get you some mentions live and in the program.

Smart Marketing Action Plan:

- Donate a popular item.
- Package your services into a big retail value.
- Negotiate for live mentions.
- Provide the program in exchange for advertising.

Chapter 7

Promotions to Increase Sales Right in Your Back Yard

We were working with the Back Yard Burger franchisees in the Knoxville area with local store marketing. In just one month each of the store managers came up with promotions that cost very little yet brought in customers.

Doggy Dog Promotion.

One clever promotion was from their Ashville franchisee who came up with the idea, "dogs eat free."Of course everyone has heard of promotions where kids eat free, but dogs, got our attention. They collect the unused hamburgers that normally would have to be thrown out. They cut them up in the bite sizes pieces and they give them to the customers' dogs when they go through the drive-thru window. The promotion is done on a specific day of the week and customers come by regularly to take advantage of the promotion. The really clever part of the promotion is that it costs nothing. They don't have to buy treats since they're using their own product.

Food And Flicks.

The single most successful promotion they did was a simple cross promotion with a Blockbuster. The Blockbuster assistant manager is a regular at Steve's (the manager) location and he was able to suggest the idea to him without having to leave the store. They traded gift certificates for their employees, who handed out a special certificate that allowed each Blockbuster customer to get a special meal deal. In just the first few weeks of the promotion, Steve generated 92 new customers. To determine if a customer was a first timer, Steve had his counter people ask each customer with the certificate if it was the first time to a Back Yard Burger? This simple question helped to determine a new customer from one that was a regular. That number will no doubt increase over the weeks following. Oddly enough, they received an additional 55 redemptions at one of their other locations further away.

Cookie Sales.

The burger bucks promotion was designed for non-profit organizations. In Ashville, they were able to get the Girl Scouts to promote a $1.00 off certificate with the purchase of cookies. Part of the arrangement was to allow the Girl Scouts to sell their cookies at their two locations. Yet the $1.00 certificates were used at all points of distribution. Only 10% of the redemptions came from the on site sales. The nice thing about this promotion is that it ties you in with a high-visibility organization and the actual discount is very slow. As a result of this effort, the Boy Scouts approached the franchisee for the same arrangement for their popcorn sales.

Kids Night.

Kids nights are always a nice way to pick up business on a slow day. The twist here is that Natalie, the franchise owner, was able to provide an inflatable "moon walk" attraction at two of her locations. Normally they would cost quite a bit, but the vendor just bought three new attractions and wanted to get the word out that they were available for rent at birthday parities and other special events. Fortunately, Natalie's two locations are on busy streets, so the vendor agreed to provide them, at two locations, every Monday for four weeks. The only cost was $50 each to cover the cost of the person to run the attraction. The vendor will pass out brochures about his moon walk attractions to the customers. Everybody wins.

Smart Marketing Action Plan:

- Look for cross promotion partners that can pass out a large number of certificates.
- Find a way to appeal to customers' emotions, like providing something for their pet.
- Work with vendors in a way that you can provide something free for your customers and at no cost to you.
- Work with nonprofit organizations in a win-win environment.

Chapter 8

Dealing with Unhappy Customers

Your first step when dealing with a difficult customer is to get yourself mentally prepared, according to Patrick J. Donadio, a Columbus, Ohio based speaker and trainer who advises leaders and organizations on improving their customer relations. Here are some of his suggestions:

Check your body posture and smile

If you are on the phone, smile with your voice. If possible, grab a pencil and paper and take brief, but specific notes. Get in the "adult" state of mind. According to Dr. Eric Burn, we behave in three modes of behavior, referred to as Transactional Analysis (TA), the child, parent and adult.

When in the "child" mode, one is very emotional. When in the "parent" mode, you act more like a parent being judgmental: If someone is not doing it "the right" way, they will be scolded. The best mode is the "adult" mode, where you focus on the facts and not the person or the behavior. Successfully dealing with difficult customers isn't hard, if you just follow a few ground rules: Understand, be understood and check for understanding.

First, seek to understand what your customer is saying, then seek to be understood. Don't blurt out "I'm sorry, I can't help you." Ask questions and listen. Even if you can't help them, asking questions and listening will help calm down the customer, build rapport and give you a better perspective.

Next, check for understanding

Let emotions run their course and then build a bridge to rational discussion. Don't forget to smile. If possible, ask permission to use the customer's name and use it. This helps calm the customer and build rapport. Also state or restate your purpose to them. For example, "My priority is to help you solve your problem." Then ask questions for clarification, to check for accuracy or to hear the information again. This tactic reinforces that you really mean what you say.

Preserve the Relationship

Once you understand your customer's problem, it's time to solve it and preserve the relationship. Ask your customer specific questions to find out exactly what he or she wants: "Why is this happening?" "What can we do about it?" Involve the customer in the solution process. Be sure you know what they want. If you are still not sure, ask again. Possible answers to the problem could be a refund, a credit or a discount on future services.

Propose a fair solution, and get the customer's support: "If I take it back and give you full credit, would that be OK with you?"

Finally, you must sell the solution by showing the customer how he or she will benefit: "If you complete the form today and mail it to us, we will still have plenty of time to get you in our next directory."

Close the Interaction in a Positive Manner

After you've worked to iron out the problems with your customer, it is important that you summarize and close the interaction in a positive manner.

First, review the agreement you reached, and use terms of mutuality when reviewing the solution. For example, "Let's both be sure of what we agreed to do." Be explicit about the steps that you promised to take and the ones that the customer agreed to perform. Finally, thank the customer for his or her time and indicate your willingness to help in the future. As soon as possible after you finish your conversation with the customer, record the information and solutions/actions on your calendar or on a form. Note each step you agreed to take and exactly when you will do them. If possible, issue a written confirmation of the agreement. This gives you another opportunity to mend the relationship. Where appropriate, make a follow-up call to the customer to see if he or she is satisfied.

Chapter 9

Think Before You Run Your Commercials

Local advertisers often times make the most basic mistakes in their messages. But none as blatant as a couple of Central Ohio car dealers. For a while there's been a very successful series of commercials by a small dealer. It's a syndicated commercial about a "trunk monkey." It's very clever and has gotten quite a bit of attention including from the local press. Then one of the largest car dealers, who have a reputation for doing silly commercials, makes reference to the small dealer's commercial.

When you're a leader in your marketplace, you don't want to draw attention to the smaller competitor. That approach simply elevates the smaller guy to the bigger guys level. If, on the other hand, your competing with a larger competitor, you want as much comparison as you can get because it does elevate you.

When you're creating a commercial on a limited budget, you need to keep several things in mind. First, you want to create a message that "sells." It's not your job to entertain the masses with your money. The job of advertising is generating customers, phone calls, or awareness. Ideally, you want to do that in a compelling way. Since there is such an abundance of advertising, you need to deliver your message in a way that is memorable. But don't let the style of your commercial interfere with the selling message.

Also make certain that the style of your commercial is appropriate for your brand. For example, there's a local jeweler who uses the hokiest TV commercial featuring his two sons and himself. When buying a product like fine jewelry there has to be a great deal of trust between the customer and the store. Is that an appropriate image for selling a high-end product? A local hospital has a commercial showing it's doctors doing goofy things. It might be attention getting but would you feel comfortable going to a hospital where the doctors have been presented in a less then professional situation? Probably not.

One of the worst commercials has to be a local car dealer who was using a disco theme in his radio commercial. The background song he chose was "Do The Hustle." At the end of the commercial you hear the lyrics sing, "do the hustle." Car dealers have bad enough reputations without reinforcing that you're going to be "hustled" at this particular dealership.

Smart Marketing Action Plan

When creating your commercial, first ask yourself the following questions:

- What is the main message you're trying to get across the audience?

- What is the image you want to portray in the community? A more technical term for this is the "position" you have in the market place. That could be the biggest, the best, the fastest, etc.

- Does the creative approach to your commercial reinforce that message or does it distract?

- Is the creative approach to your commercial that you're considering in conflict with the position you have in the marketplace?

- Are you using enough repetition of a commercial (frequency) to allow your message to really break though and make some impact. As a rule, the same person needs to hear or see your commercial at least six times before they begin to remember it.

Chapter 10

Charity Begins At Work

Businesses are deluged with requests for donations by many charity organizations. Making donations to all these worthy causes is difficult for many small businesses and as a result it's likely that the charity group gets frustrated with its efforts. So, if you're put in charge of a fund raising program for your organization, think of the effort as you would a revenue generator for your business.

What's in it for me?

Before approaching all the local businesses for donations, develop your fund raiser so that the local business will actually get some tangible benefits from it. An ad in your program book or bulletin is tantamount to asking for a donation. It's has very little real advertising value for that business. So think of something you can do that generates donations for you while at the same time drives customers into the small business to buy.

On Sight Even

One powerful way is to have an event at the location of the small business. Your donation comes from a percentage of new sales generated as a result of your event. Your organization is responsible for promoting the event. Have flyers printed and distributed, get announcements on local radio station and newspapers. You can even ask non-competitive businesses to display posters and put up a message about your event on their marquee signs. Since you're promoting a non-profit event, it's possible to get those posters and flyers printed, free. Simply offer to put a notice at the bottom of your printed matter that XYZ printing company donated it.

When talking to a business owner about doing such a promotion, think of it from his or her perspective. Offer to do it on a Thursday night. You don't want to tie up their weekend business but you don't want a Monday night either since that's generally the slowest night. Also, choose a type of business that everyone can go to. A restaurant works well for this or possibly a car wash. Each of these has a high enough profit margin that they can afford to donate perhaps 50 percent of the take that night. You can even offer to back out their normal sales so that they only donate the amount based on the increase in sales that your organization has provided.

Customers would come in that night and buy at the regular price. Not only do you generate some new customers, you do so without having to provide them a discount. When you discount to bring a new customer, many times that customer won't return unless there is another discount available. However, with this promotion, the customers come in because they are supporting your cause. They pay full price and have an opportunity to experience the food and service of your host restaurant. This is a big benefit to the restaurant, which you can bring up when you present this idea.

Lastly, suggest to your host restaurant that special bounce-back coupons are provided to all the participants who support the event. This could be a standard "dollars off" type coupon however, the amount of the coupon is donated to your group and the customer pays full price. It might say something like, "Thank you for supporting our fund raiser. Come back to this restaurant in the next two weeks, order any entrée and $2.00 will be donated to our organization."

Chapter 11

Getting In The Door To Make Your Pitch

When you're having trouble getting in to see your prospects, you need to get a little creative. That's exactly what Dan did to promote his Figaro's franchise pizza restaurant in Eugene, Oregon. We were training the franchisees in Eugene on how to set up cross promotions. In the beginning stages of implementing cross promotions, we suggest they start with people they know, in particular their own customers. The advantages are that the prospect is coming to you and they are already familiar with your product and the quality of your service.

However, some of the biggest cross promotion opportunities in their trading area happened to be businesses with managers or owners who were not his customer. So, Dan suggested that if the decision maker isn't coming to him, he would have to go visit the decision maker. Of course the problem there is that business people don't like to receive sales pitches. Dan solved that problem by simply taking him a pizza with him on each visit. He would show up about 11:30 with a large pizza and in just about every instance, was welcomed with open arms. His goal was to deliver one pizza a day to a key business in his area. In just one month, he made numerous contacts and set up many promotions.

We had a similar experience several years ago when a local bank manger came to visit our office. He brought with him a jar filled with gourmet jelly beans. It was just enough to get our attention. As a result, that branch manager had the opportunity to ask us some questions about our business and banking needs. That cold call, resulted in that bank refinancing the mortgage on our office building.

Capture attention

To be successful on a contact, first have a way to capture the attention of the prospect. Hot pizza, jelly beans or other fun type "peace offerings" can be just the ticket to get you past a gate keeper. Keep it fun and not too expensive. Dropping off a catalogue or promotional materials would not fall into this category. That comes later.

Sometimes it helps to call first. Generally, it's very difficult to reach decision makers by phone but you can use a telephone call to determine the days and time your prospect is likely to be in. If the opportunity allows, see if you can gather some key information about your prospect from the receptionist; including the name of his or her personal secretary, official title, hobbies, and pet peeves.

Prepare several key questions

Next, be prepared should you get an opportunity to talk with a decision maker. You'll want to have several key questions prepared so that you can determine in just a few minutes, if this prospect has potential. If the prospect looks promising, offer to stop by when he or she has more time to learn about how you can provide the "benefit" he or she is looking for. Try to nail that person down to a specific time for the second visit.

Lastly, get a "thank you" card in the mail that day. You want that card to show up within a few days of your initial visit. This card helps to reinforce that initial contact and remind the prospect of your future visit.

Don't rush the close

Don't try to do too much too soon. Most selling efforts have a natural rhythm to them and if you try the rush the process, the prospect becomes defensive. That's why it's important to work a number of new prospects all the time. Have a steady pipeline of potential new business every week.

SMART MARKETING ACTION PLAN:

- Show up bearing gifts, but not expensive ones.
- Be prepared to leverage the few minutes you get with the decision maker.
- Try calling first for conducting some initial research.
- Don't try to do too much in the first visit.
- Follow up with a thank-you note right away.

Chapter 12

Business Lunch Etiquette

Since many business meetings are conducted over lunch, you don't want to jeopardize your chances of success with an etiquette faux pas. Here are several basic tips to make sure your client is focused on your message and not your mess.

Choose an appropriate venue. If you have the ability to select the restaurant, choose one that is conducive to conducting business. You will want a place that's reasonably quiet where your client will feel comfortable sharing information with you. Ideally, you want to choose a place that takes reservations so you don't have to wait too long for a table. If not, you may want to arrive early enough so you can be seated before your client arrives. Make sure your server knows you're there to conduct business. You want prompt service but you also want to be left alone once the business conversation starts. Tipping the server in advance can help. You also want to make sure you're seated in a quiet area of the restaurant. If time permits, you might want to do some advance research on the restaurant. This is no time to take chances.

Choose an appropriate menu. Make sure the selections available are appropriate. Find out in advance if your client or prospect has any dietary restrictions. He or she may be on a certain diet so you want to make sure there are plenty of choices. Also, when choosing your meal, choose something that won't be too messy and is easy to negotiate when talking. Try to seat yourself in a position of authority, with your back to the wall and your prospects' back to the main area of the restaurant. This way there is likely to be less distractions.

Manners. Once the food arrives, don't start eating until your guest starts. If you need to excuse yourself, place your napkin on your chair. When eating a roll or slice of bread, pull off a small piece with your hand and butter it using a knife. Don't take a bite then place the remains back on your plate. Once the meal is finished and you're ready to leave, place your napkin neatly on the table. Inform your server in advance that you want the check. This avoids awkwardness once it arrives. Or better yet, give your server your credit card ahead of time so you don't have to deal with it during your meeting. Tip 20%. Turn your cell phone off or in vibrate mode. When you're finished with your meal, place your silverware close together at an angle on your plate. This is a signal to your server that you're finished. However, try not to finish before your guest. It looks strange to have your place cleared before your guest is finished with his or her meal. .

SMART MARKETING ACTION PLAN:

For a successful business lunch:
- Choose a quiet restaurant.
- Find out in advance of any dietary restrictions.
- Make sure your server knows you're there for business.
- Tip in advance.
- Order non-messy food.

Chapter 13

Look For Bargains to Save Money on Overhead

When running a small business or home office, you want to save as much money as you can on expenses. There are ways to cut the cost of doing business if you look for them. Sometimes there are hidden costs behind the supplies and equipment you use in your office. For example, a brand new ink jet printer does not really cost that much to buy. Depending on your needs you can get a state-of-the-art color ink jet printer for less than $200. The only problem in that a set of ink cartridges often cost over $50. You've doubled the cost of that printer in just four sets of ink cartridge replacements. Sometimes you can refill them yourself but that can be time consuming and messy and not always the best use of your time.

In our office we use a slightly older model of ink jet printer. Now we buy them used on Ebay, usually for under $100. When one breaks down, we toss it out. Fortunately, there are generic cartridges for that printer. The branded ones cost as much as $25 each. But we've discovered sources that can get us the black cartridges for only $2.50 each and the $3.50 for the color ones. That includes shipping in quantities of 10 or more. Even though this printer isn't the fastest, the quality of the final printed pieces is very high. The cost of each sheet is a fraction of what it would have cost on a newer style of printer. We also found out that by looking around, especially on line, you can find ink jet photo quality paper, 8 ½ x 11 for a nickel a sheet.

Another area where you can save money by shopping on line is specialty printing. Recently we needed 500 engraved invitations, with matching envelopes for a special business luncheon. After searching, we discovered a wedding invitation company on the web, who was discontinuing a style of formal invitations that were perfect for our needs. They custom printed and expressed shipped the entire job in less than 10 days. The final cost was one-third of something similarly quoted by several printers closer to home. By thinking outside the normal office brand mentality we got a beautifully engraved invitation that commanded attention from those cordially invited.

It also helps to think ahead to those items you'll need to buy in the future. Some times you can buy those items at significant discounts by shopping in the off season or just after the main buying season. For example, we carry a supply of different greeting cards in the office so they're available when they're needed. These would include birthday, congratulations, get well soon, condolences and so on. When our local shops and discount places run specials on their cards, we stock up, knowing that we might not need them for up to a year. The cost of the cards is about a third of retail and we always have them in stock when we need them.

Looking for bargains is a good way to keep costs down. At the same time, you want to make sure the discounted merchandise you're buying is the same quality as the full priced one. It's not a deal unless it fully serves your needs. There's a time to cut back and a time when there are other considerations aside from price. Use some common sense.

Smart Marketing Action Plan:

- Check out generic products to see if they will work for you.
- Think ahead for items you might need in the future and buy in bulk when you can.
- Look for bargains to keep costs down.

Chapter 14

Big Advantages in Using a Professional Presenter

(Part 1 of 2)

When your company plans a convention or major meeting, consider using professional speakers instead of a business or industry insider. According to Nancy Lauterbach, the owner of a speaker bureau in Phoenix, Arizona, "Using an outside professional speaker can lend a much higher level of credibility to your corporate message ... one that you can't get when your own people are presenting that information." There are many other advantages in using a professional speaker including:

Entertainment Value

Unfortunately, most speakers are boring. If the audience is not engaged, they simply won't remember the message. A professional speaker on the other hand, knows how to engage the audience. Better speakers use anecdotes and humor to engage their audience. Once they've bonded, the underlying message is more likely to be remembered and implemented.

Plausible Deniability

An outside speaker can deliver information that may be too harsh when coming from internal management. By relieving management the "bad guy" image, suggestions and new information will more likely be accepted. The audience needs to hear it, but may not want to hear it unless the presenter has credibility. For example, many franchise organizations bring us in to talk about local store marketing. One of the key success elements for the franchisee or local store owner is the need to take responsibility for the implementation of marketing within a few miles of their location — not relying on corporate to do it all for them. As you can imagine, this is not a popular message, but one that has to be delivered. When we do it, it's more likely to be accepted because we are from the outside. We also offer specific tactics that are very simple to execute locally.

Follow Up Potential

Most of the better professional speakers, while not household names, have some degree of notoriety. In many cases they are authors of books on their subject. These books are often available at a significant discount when purchased in bulk by the client. The client provides the books to their attendees as a way of reinforcing the message from the convention or conference. Some speakers can even provide custom handouts, audio programs or even video programs to supplement the theme or message.

Specific Expertise

There are many speakers available. As a speaker bureau representative, Nancy Lauterbach's job is to match the needs of clients with available speakers. Subjects, availabilities and fees are areas where a good speaker bureau can help you sort through the thousands of options. But, while you can get a professional speaker from $500 to $10,000, you often get what you pay for. The bureau has videos to review and often has video clips available on their websites. Another way to identify desirable speakers is through "speaker showcases" sponsored by speaker bureaus.

Chapter 15

When Not To Use a Celebrity Speaker

(Part 2 of 2)

Many organizations use celebrity speakers at their conventions or events. This is not always the right approach for providing your audience the best program. The only reason to consider paying a premium for a celebrity speaker is to help get attendance at your program. Using a celebrity as a "draw" can be very effective if your attendees are not required to attend. For example, The Consumers' Choice Award of Indianapolis is a Street Fighter

Marketing client who needed to create an event that would attract hundreds of local business people to a luncheon. This event was as designed to explain the benefits of buying their licensing program.

To create extra excitement, Bob Eubanks, the former host of the Newlywed Game, was hired to be the emcee at the recognition luncheon. We also hired Mr. Eubanks as their celebrity spokesperson in all of their advertising which included billboards, an extensive newspaper schedule and radio. He did a super job at the luncheon and the banquet hall was packed. He was also available to have his picture taken with all the award recipients.

This situation was the right one for using a celebrity. Mr. Eubanks was a great draw for this particular target audience and he was a joy to work with. He showed funny video clips of the Newlywed Game and shared some of the behind the scene stories. But most importantly, he tied his message into the theme of the luncheon. Unfortunately, most celebrities won't really do that for you. They say what they want to say on their terms, and they're often very difficult to work with.

If you have an event where your audience members are required to attend, a celebrity may not be the way to go. Often times, sports figures are brought in to add excitement to the event. The problem is that most of them are very poor speakers. On the other hand, if you were to hire a reputable professional speaker, there are several advantages:

1. A professional speaker costs less then a celebrity speaker.

2. Your audience is more likely to get usable information.

3. Your audience is more likely to get a presentation that is compelling and entertaining.

4. A professional speaker is generally more willing to tailor his or her remarks specifically to your audience.

So, if you're thinking of bringing in a big name celebrity to your event, make sure the high fees and low content you get from such a presenter does the job you want it to do. If you decide you want more bang for your buck and you have a captive audience, consider hiring a speaking professional with a strong message and a powerful presentation.

Chapter 16

When To Help Promote Your Competition

Sometimes you get more by helping your competitor. That may sound strange, but there are special situations where promoting your competitor will help increase your sales. One example of this is the "in the loop" promotion. The first time we used this type of promotion was when we were part owners of a nightclub. Knowing most of our customers, even the "regulars" did a certain amount of bar hopping. We knew club was one of perhaps twenty that they could visit in a given night.

The idea behind "in the loop" was to create an association of bar owners with whom we had a good relationship. There were six of us in all. We had a special certificate created that was given to our customers when they left our club. The other five establishments would do the same. The offer on the promotional piece was good at any of the other five operations for that night. This would provide an incentive for those customers, leaving to go elsewhere, to choose one of the nightclubs in the loop. So, as customers would leave one of the 14 other clubs not in the program, our group would capture that customer.

Each club owner could track the results because the customer was redeeming a certificate. Once a customer went to any of the six participating "loop" clubs, there were incentives to keep them in the loop.

Therefore the market share of the six increased, as did their sales.

A more recent example of this came up when a regional fast food hamburger restaurant, the top franchisee in the chain, found out a new competitor was moving into the market. This hamburger place competes toe-to-toe with a national hamburger franchise down the street. The national hamburger franchise, like the regional competitor, is on the short list of one of highest volume units in the chain.

Now they both face competition from a new player. How can they work together? Here are a few of the suggestions we gave them:

1. During the grand opening week of the new competitor, the two will hand out certificates to their customers promoting the other's restaurant. The purpose is to keep people from trying the new place.

2. Shut down for one lunch day-part (shift). That's right, shut down. Then put up a banner that says, "In Honor of our new neighbor, we're closed. Go visit them." With both high volume places shut down, the only place will be the new place. Since it's likely they weren't expecting to have a 100% of the market share that lunch, customers will probably be waiting a very long time for their food. They will get annoyed at the slow service. They'll get angry. And, since their first experience with this new competitor is likely to be negative, they may vow never to return.

Chapter 17

Steps to Success

In his book, *The Seven Steps to Success: A common-sense guide to succeed in specialty coffee*, Greg Ubert outlines some very specific business concepts and strategies that would apply to nearly any business. Mr. Ubert is the founder and president of CrimsonCup® Coffee & Tea based in Columbus, Ohio. CrimsonCup® roasts specialty grade coffees and supplies independent coffeehouses throughout the country. But what makes this organization unique is that they don't merely wholesale coffee to their retail customers. They teach them how to be successful selling specialty coffee.

Mr. Ubert urges his coffee retailers to know what their business is about before they get started. To be successful, you must know your focus. For example, to be successful in a coffeehouse, he strongly advises them to stay away from sandwiches and soups. The amount of time and resources devoted to food items would interfere with focusing on the elements that provide a coffeehouse a competitive edge in its neighborhood. What sets a good coffeehouse apart and makes it profitable is serving great espresso-based drinks. That's their "bread and butter." Likewise, Mr. Ubert urges his retailers to avoid drip coffee, because it forces the coffeehouse to compete directly with food establishments. Drip coffee has lower profit, lower perceived value and, generally, requires free refills. Remember, people can buy coffee at restaurants and grocery stores. They go to coffeehouse to enjoy something they cannot get at home: a great espresso-based drink.

The universal lesson here is: regardless of the type of business you're in, you must really know where you make your profits and what makes you unique in the marketplace. What is the "equivalent" in your business to the espresso-based coffee drinks? Ask yourself:

Which products or services you offer, make you unique?

Which products or services you offer allow you to command a premium price?

Which products and services you offer will motivate your customers to buy from you instead of your competition?

One of the seven steps in the book is: Focus on Customer Service. This is a key to any business success. Part of customer service is to let your customers know about those special products and services that you offer. In the coffeehouse environment, the suggestion is to get a drip coffee drinker to try an espresso-based drink. Your employees should try the special of the day. Nothing sounds better to customers than to hear that the staff person praises the very product that is being suggested. If you encourage your employees to try the special, they are more likely to offer it to a customer.

Another suggested way to subtly add-on to the sale is when a customer orders a cup of drip coffee, the server should ask, "Do you want room for cream?" If they say yes, then he or she should ask if they like their drink sweet. From there it's just one small step to move that person to the profitable espresso-based drink. The bottom line here is that those people in your business who come in contact with your customers should be asking questions. They need to find out more details about what they really want and need, instead of just assuming that what they order is good enough. In many cases, those customers may not even know you offer certain types of products and services. By not making them of aware of your best values, you are doing the customer and your business a disservice.

Chapter 18

A Tale of Two Banks

It was the best of banks, it was the worst of banks, it was managed with wisdom, it was managed with foolishness, it was the epoch of customer service, it was the epoch of lousy service…

Tis a classic tale: bigger is not always better. Customer service and attention to detail should be your highest priority when it comes to your money. Finding a financial institution that combines the best services and features can be to your benefit in saving money on fees as well as time management in the processing of transactions. As we compare the details between smaller locally owned or independent banks and the larger corporate or publicly owned banks you can educate yourself about what matters most to you and your business.

Since ATM's or debit cards have become popular the need for multiple branch locations has become almost obsolete. You can access your money virtually anywhere. In addition, the internet provides instant on line banking information to you at your desk. This modern technology allows you to complete transactions without having to drive around town and provides even the smallest banks with an equal playing field for convenience. Find a locally owned bank that offers these amenities and combines technology with personal attention on a local level.

The Best of Banks

An example of this philosophy is Country Club Bank in Kansas

City. A leader in providing exceptional customer service this bank invests in their clients. Even though they only have 12 locations, they provide the modern and advanced ability to bank on line. Offering all of the most current internet technology and employing the finest people to make each transaction effortless, Country Club Bank retains customers by treating each account as if they were their only account. Whether banking in person or from your desk, Country Club Bank supports the customer with the best possible service. With a mission statement that says, "Built on Relationships. Investing in You" Country Club Bank empowers their employees to do what is right for each customer. This bank assigns a personal banker to each customer so that any issues can be resolved in one phone call to a familiar voice- a trusted liaison between the client and the bank itself. This business relationship offers advantages you can not get with a bigger bank. Country Club Bank does such a good job at spoiling their customers that many of them keep their accounts open and active despite the fact that they have moved out of the local service area. They make it so easy to bank with them, that there is no need to bank anywhere else.

The Worst of Banks

In contrast, larger banks often fall short of seeing your business as important. Getting lost in the shuffle can make your experience less than desirable. For example, a client of ours has been complaining about the lack of genuine customer service from Huntington Bank in Columbus, Ohio. With over 45 locations this bank is on every corner, but unfortunately, their under-staffed drive thru lanes at peak times, ridiculous fees for minor details, and a toll free customer service line that is automated and impersonal makes for a frustrating experience. The hassle of working with Huntington Bank has caused our client to look elsewhere for a bank who will appreciate their business. A phone call to Landis Bryson, Help Desk Supervisor with Huntington Bank gave us insight to the problem with bigger banks. Policies are set in stone and despite the individual situation are not negotiable. "The customer is king" mentality does not apply to bigger banks, as was obvious with Ms. Bryson who was just handling callers rather than helping them. Huntington Bank has not empowered their employees to make a difference in the day to day banking business experience. Being bigger in this case is not a bonus.

So, when it comes to the smaller bank…It is a far, far better bank that I have used, than I have used before; it is far, far better service that I gotten than I have ever known.

Smart Marketing Action Plan:

Lessons Learned:

- Offers technology that lets your customers use your services more effectively and conveniently.
- Provide knowledgeable people to serve your customers.
- Give customer service that puts your customers' needs first.

Chapter 19

Gaining New Insights About Your Business, From The Outside

You can get deeper and more valuable input from your customers or clients by creating an advisory group or outside board of directors, according to Jeff Blackman a Chicago, Illinois based speaker, author, success coach, broadcaster and lawyer. Mr. Blackman suggests that you call several of your key customers or clients and ask them to be part of your advisory council. Contact folks who know you, like you and trust you. A big advantage of working with an outside advisory group is that they can also be brutally honest with you, your leadership team, sales team, etc. You choose how often you want your group to meet, whether it's quarterly, semi-annually, or annually.

Mr. Blackman speaks from experience as he has had the pleasure to facilitate numerous advisory councils or outside boards for a variety of clients. Since he had no bias or pre-disposition, he asked the tough questions that his clients might be hesitant to ask. He then counsels his clients to listen very carefully with an open mind. Blackman unequivocally urges, repeatedly recommends and strongly stresses that they not convert this meeting into a sales pitch for their latest product or service. When we facilitate a similar meeting for our clients, we like to send out an advanced agenda. This gets the participants thinking about the high priority areas. It also keeps them focused at the meeting on key subjects that will best benefit from this groups' expertise and experiences. The key is to create a healthy and honest dialogue with your clients or customers, so together you can best determine how to grow your respective businesses. At these meetings, you should emphasize some simple messages

- This is a time for honesty not hesitancy.
- This is a time for truth not being timid.
- This is a time for candor not caution.

You should expect the exchanges to be lively, spirited and even emotional. Let your clients and their customers generally value the experience. It strengthens relationships and creates deeper levels of understanding. It also drives future business. Also, be sure to pamper your advisors or council members. Spoil them. Treat them like the VIPs that they are. This means that you should pay for their airfare, transportation, hotel, food, gifts, etc.

Your follow up effort after the meeting is also very important. Within one to two weeks of the initial dialogue, be sure to: send participants thank you notes and send copies of the "team picture" taken at the event, send a press release to a "board member's" local newspaper, highlighting their participation send a hardcopy or e-mail document that recaps the major issues discussed, as well as the game plan for future discussions, action steps or resolutions honor any commitment or deliverables.

The only risk to your credibility, is if you merely listen and choose to do nothing. For additional information and 11 more powerful strategies for gaining insights from the outside, send an e-mail to: **jeff@jeffblackman.com** with the subject heading: "Council" and he'll send you a free copy via e-mail.

Chapter 20

Winning Words

If you want long-term business-growth success, instead of a quick path to extinction, stress the value and significance of words and language, according to Jeff Blackman a Chicago, Illinois based speaker, author, success coach, broadcaster and lawyer. Here are some of Blackman's examples: While at O'Hare Airport, Blackman overheard one businessman say to another, "What should I say? Can you give me magic words?" This fellow was searching for words of wisdom. He wanted to avoid language losers. Why? Because the words, phrases and questions you use really do matter. Especially, in a marketing, sales, service or persuasive message. This point was driven home by a bunch of first-graders.

When the Blackmans were celebrating their youngest daughter Amanda's 7th birthday in her school classroom, his wife served chocolate cupcakes, while their other daughter Brittany, and he were in charge of "drink distribution." To the first group of four kids, he asked, "Would you like apple juice or citrus cooler?" Each, with a look of confusion, cautiously responded, "Apple juice."

Brittany said, "Daddy, nobody wants citrus cooler." That's when it hit him. He exclaimed, "Brittany, how could they? Why would they? Who the heck even knows what citrus cooler is?" I said, "Brittany, I used ill-conceived language that didn't appeal to their dominant buying motives for risk, excitement and adventure." Brittany then said what she often says, "Daddy, you're very strange!"

He then said, "Brit, watch this!" He asked 15 more children: "Which would you like regular apple juice or yummy green bug juice?" Their eyes bulged! Cheeks puffed! Smiles erupted! And, 14 of 15 exclaimed, "Gimme yummy green bug juice!"

Here's another example: Gus, a salesperson for a personal-improvement website was trying to woo Blackman to advertise on his site. In his voice-mail messages, Gus assured him, "Jeff, you'll make big bucks just like your friends in the industry." He was skeptical, but set-up a brief phone meeting. A time and date was scheduled for Gus to reach Blackman on his private line. Gus called. Twenty hours early!

Blackman told him that he was chatting with a client on another line, could he please call back at the scheduled time. He said dejectedly, "Okay, I was just hoping to pitch you now." (Hmmm. He wasn't going to assess his goals and needs, he was "pitching.") The next day, Blackman waited for the phone to ring. It didn't. Gus blew-off the phone-date. Ninety minutes later, his private line rang. It was Gus. "Gus, is everything okay? I expected your call at 2:00." He replied, "Oh, I didn't call because we're moving our offices and I lost track of time." (Gus sells self-improvement and he can't keep track of time!). He then said, "Let's make this quick. This will work for you. You deserve to pay $600."

Blackman exclaimed, "I deserve to pay?" He said, "Ummm, maybe that's not the right word." (No kidding!) Gus then tried to flatter him, when he boldly declared, "Jeff, I've already gotten commitments from other superstars like you. (It didn't work. I ain't a big fan of fawning and insincere praise).When I asked, "Who?" He started name-dropping. Amazingly, every name he dropped, he mispronounced. Blackman politely ended the conversation, by requesting he send this "superstars" list so he could confirm the results. He assured him, "You'll get it today."It never came.

SMART MARKETING ACTION PLAN

Jeff Blackman has created a list of 189 power words and profit phrases. Here's a sneak-preview of 18 of them. Use them in your advertising: proven, partnership, lightest, new, bargain, compact, research, exclusive, prestige, priceless, free, craftsmanship, trouble-free, investment, solid, biggest, quality, contemporary.

Chapter 21

Resisting Costly Hiring Mistakes

Resistance to change, when it comes to your hiring practices can be a very costly practice, according to Barry Shamis, President of Selecting Winners, a Seattle, Washington based recruiting company.

The History

The common wisdom is simply the process and techniques that business people have used for hiring. It has been the same way for so long that most people have come to assume it is the right way. Look at how most managers start hiring. They are promoted to a management position and one of the first things they have to do is hire someone. They are given no training or guidance so they usually do what was done to them. Whatever process was used when they were hired is what they emulate to hire their first person. The process, good or bad, perpetuates indefinitely.

This is why bad habits and practices have proliferated when it comes to hiring. And the bad practices have been around for so long that people believe them to be right. Thus, the "common wisdom" dominates and your hiring effectiveness just never gets better.

Resistance to change

"I have always done it this way," "Everyone else does it this way," "This is just the way it is," "My results are no different than anyone else." These are just a few of the typical statements Mr. Shamis hears when he talks to clients about their hiring practices. Too often they dig in their heels and defend the status quo instead of looking for a better way.

During his three recent presentations he asked each group what their biggest business problem was. As always, the answer was recruiting, hiring and keeping good employees. This, by the way, is the standard answer he gets with almost every group.

The sad part is that when he queries them on what they are doing about it the answers are usually quite feeble. If lack of sales was your biggest problem, you would move heaven and earth to fix the problem. Why is it then that you do not move heaven and earth to fix your hiring problem.

So, Shamis urges companies to embrace change and try something different. One of the Chief Executives who was in his presentation told Shamis that he spends between two and three hours a day, everyday, recruiting for his company. He told the group a story about how impressed candidates were when they realized the first contact from the company was from the CEO. Now there is a strategy that is effective.

Another effective strategy that we have used at Street Fighter Marketing is to use an outside recruiting consultant to do all the initial interview. The consultant reviews the resumes, sets up the initial appointment and then narrows the field down to three or four of the best candidates. This saves us a tremendous amount of time and costs a fraction of using an employment agency which typically charges a big percentage of the first year salary of the recruit

It is time to take the common wisdom and challenge it. If you are unhappy with the results you are getting using the same old tools and techniques, try something new. Don't allow the narrow thinkers and the naysayers to stop you from recruiting and hiring the best employees. For more information about Selecting Winners visit them online at www.selectingwinners.com.

Chapter 22

Good Service
Closes The Sale

Recently Marc was shopping for a new car. He narrowed down the basic type of car that he wanted, and there were about six different brands that fit into hit list. Marc took the time to test drive each car at least once and talked with each of the sales people several times. Each of the six different brands of car performed roughly the same; so, the determining factor was the effort of the sales person and the quality of the dealership. His choice was made and the car was purchased. Infiniti of Columbus was the dealership that worked hardest for the business. Even though their product did not have a competitive edge over the competition, they won by going out of their way to put together an offering that was superior. The elements that tipped the sale in their favor was:

Good price

They were able to bring the price down just a little lower than the competition.

Good sales effort

They were persistent without being pushy. This is a fine line to deal with. You want to make sure that you keep in front of the customer without turning the customer off. This effort has to be adjusted to the personality of the customer. Since Marc has a sales and marketing background, a more persistent effort was needed than perhaps the average customer.

Good service

This dealership has a reputation for providing very good service. Even though they weren't the most convenient location, Marc felt that should he have any problems or requests they would be dealt with promptly and properly.

If you see a product or service that is perceived by your potential customers as basically the same as your competition, you need to figure out a way of gaining an edge. Determine if any of the following will help you win the sale over your competition.

Add-ons

You may have additional items or services that have a high profit margin or cost you very little that you can include as a "sweetener" to make your package better. For example, when Marc was talking with the car dealership, they wouldn't go any lower on the price but they were able to provide an extended warranty for about half of what they normally would. Even so, I'm sure they'll make some extra money on it, but even if they just broke even on this add-on, it was the final extra that got them the sale.

Effort

You can offer to provide your customer something that they don't expect. When Marc had already agreed to buy the car, he mentioned that the one thing that concerned him initially with the dealership was their location was on the other side of town. The General Sales Manager, Steve, as it turned out lives close to our office and offered to pick the car up and drop it off if needed. Keep in mind that this was offered after the deal was signed. This level of service, above and beyond, is a great way to get word of mouth exposure.

Follow up

After the sale, be sure to thank your customer for their business. This effort only takes a moment of your time but helps cement the relationship. It helps with referrals and repeat business, plus should there ever be a problem that could potentially hurt the relationship, you stand a better chance of getting the opportunity to make it right.

Chapter 23

When The Joke's On You

When dealing with clients, a number of situations can crop up that can either help you reinforce your relationship or do damage. New York City based author and speaker, Leil Lowndes, offers tips and techniques for avoiding such a faux pas.

What do you do when someone tells you the same joke — again!? I'm sure you've had this conundrum: You're chatting with a friend or colleague, and they start repeating a joke or story they've told you before. Yikes, now you have a tough choice:

1) Do you interrupt and say they've told you before? Nah, that's rude.

2) Do you let them continue with their joke, and then fake a laugh? Nah, that's insincere. (Besides, halfway through, they might remember that they told it to you before.)

Now they feel foolish and think you're pandering them.) So what's a civilized person to do?

Here's your salvation. Simply let them finish the story and then say, "That's a GREAT story!" (This is appropriate whether you heard it or not.) Your reaction pleases them, and you're freed from being rude or faking a reaction. But, what if, after their story, they remember you've heard it before? They may ask why you let them continue. No problem. Simply say, "I enjoyed the story so much the first time that I wanted to hear it again!" Dale Irvin, a Downers Grove, Illinois based comedian and speaker, likes to let the person tell the entire joke or story. Even though he may have heard it numerous times, Dale is a student of humor and likes to discover new twists and approaches. So if someone says, "— stop me if you've heard this" he never does. He also feels that allowing someone to tell their anecdote or joke helps you bond with that person.

Another issue from time to time, is when a client or colleague tells you a joke or story that is off color or derogatory toward a religious or ethnic group. The danger in simply going along with it or politely laughing is that you could damage your reputation, even if you don't share the story tellers' view points. Unfortunately, not doing something is this situation is dangerous for you.

Dale has two possible approaches to this type of situation. The first is to act like you didn't hear it and, before a split second passes, change the subject. Say anything — the more irrelevant the better. The second (which she feels is the better approach) is, while they're telling it, and you see where it's going, interrupt as though you had something interesting to add to a previous (innocent) subject. While you're talking, listen for their humiliated gulp if when it dawns on them what happened.

The reverse is also true

That is, be very careful about the stories and jokes you tell. Even if the other person is laughing, you never know how they're really feeling on the inside. Unless the joke or story is obviously self deprecating, stay away from any ethnic, religious, gender or other groups that may be insulted by your story. Even if the person you're sharing the story with genuinely likes it, he or she may share that with someone who is offended. If the offended party ties the original story back you, your reputation and credibility could suffer permanent damage.

Chapter 24

How To Compete on Price

Your competition sells good stuff; you sell good stuff. Their service is acceptable; your service is acceptable. Their prices are competitive; your prices are competitive. In other words, the buyer looks at your package and the competitor's package and sees parity, along the product dimension and company dimension. However, there are some ways you can gain an edge, according to Tom Reilly, a professional speaker and author of *Value Added Selling*.

The same product, from the same company, from two different salespeople is two different solutions altogether. Mr. Reilly shares the example of two major companies who asked how much value their salespeople bring to the table and discovered that 35-37% of the value customers receive comes from the people with whom they do business.

Ask yourself, if you left your company tomorrow and went to work for a really good competitor, how much business would you take with you? If your answer is "little" or "none", Mr. Reilly suggests that you're not bringing much value to the customer.

When your products are similar or the same suppliers' services rival each other, the only thing left to differentiate a solution is the salesperson. Ask yourself these questions:

How much are you worth to the customer?

If you couldn't argue that your service was any better than the competition, how would you sell?

57

If you couldn't rely on product differentiation, what would you use as an advantage?

What if you have only yourself left to sell? You must be able to answer this question for the customer, "Why should the buyer want to do business with you as a salesperson?" You are the "product" over which you have the most control. You may not be able to do anything about your product's quality or your company's service level, but you can do something about your performance. One study found that the salesperson's competence is the number one factor accounting for overall customer satisfaction. All other things being equal, would the customer pay to do business with you, as a salesperson? To increase your value to the customer, do the following.

Study

Become a serious student of your profession. Increase the value of your knowledge. Study the market, your company, the customer, your products, and your profession. Become an expert. Learn so much about your craft that the customer can't afford not to do business with you. Become the benchmark by which all other salespeople are judged.

Follow up

The number one complaint buyers have about salespeople is a lack of follow-up. Guarantee your follow-up. Advise buyers that this is part of your value added. Assure them that you will be there after the sale to guarantee their complete satisfaction with your solution. Promise them accessibility before, during, and after the sale. Promise a lot, but always deliver more than what you promise.

Seek to add value, not cost. Diligently look for ways to add value with your performance. The customer must perceive you as a profit center, not a cost center. Help the customer achieve greater efficiency and higher productivity. Help the buyer gain maximum performance from your solution. Work as hard to keep the business as you did to get the business. Look for ways to re-create value at every turn.

For information log on to www.tomreillytraining.com.

Chapter 25

Converting Complaints to Compliments

Customer complaints offer opportunities to make customers feel important, to feel indebted to you and to validate your integrity, According to David Allen Yoho a Louisville, Kentucky based speaker and trainer. They can strengthen your relationship. The result of a complaint can be positive even when you've told them "no" The customer might actually be glad they had the problem because of how you responded.

Although complaints are born from a variety of reasons and are communicated with a huge variance in tone and intensity, a complaint is always a request. Your challenge is to identify what the individual wants (the request) without being distracted by their behavior. The challenge is: upset people rarely express themselves well.

Customers can be rude, profane, mean, deceitful, racist or sexist. Sometimes, it seems that punishing you is more important than resolving the problem. It's easy to respond with righteous indignation but you'll only make the problem worse. Anyone can serve reasonable customers; only those with exceptional customer focus, masterful skills and self-control can serve unreasonable customers.

Although it's unpleasant to hear people vent, listening actively without judgment will enhance your credibility and drain their venom. The worst mistake you can make at this point is to fuel their emotion by interrupting, giving advice or debating. Telling them to calm down can have the same effect as feeding them a grenade. Reacting in kind to anger, hurtful judgments or foul language only intensifies their wrath.

Here are some key initiatives that will diffuse their unhappiness, identify the right course, promote understanding and help you exceed their expectations.

Consider their complaint a favor

Research proves that most people don't notify you when they're unhappy. Thank them for taking the time to let you know about their dissatisfaction. Apologize for any inconvenience or offense. A humble attitude will usually disarm them and earn their respect.

Express your intent to resolve the issue in a timely manner

When the customer continues to vent, affirm them and reinforce your intent. Example: "You have every right to be angry and I'm happy to listen to whatever you have to say. With your permission, I'd like to get started fixing this mess."

If you weren't the individual who caused the complaint, assume responsibility anyway. Assessing blame won't make them feel better or make you look better. Be the company. Place your ego behind the customer's welfare.

Too often, companies attempt to buy the customer's affection with gifts or refunds. That may not alleviate the customer's primary concern and it could be an insult. A sincere apology often means more to them than a gift. You might ask them how they'd like to see the situation resolved. Interestingly, the customer often asks for less than you're willing to offer. The intent isn't to take advantage of them; it's to provide satisfaction based on their values, not yours.

You might want to offer them more than one solution. This offers some ownership in the resolution. When the customer requests something unreasonable or unacceptable (now or at any time), avoid using "can't" or "won't" Do advise them quickly and directly when you're not going to meet a request. Examples: "I'd love to do that" or "I wish I could" Then, offer one or more positive alternatives.

Obtain a satisfaction commitment to the solution before you take action. If you don't have the authority to satisfy them or if you need more information before you can decide what to do, advise them of your process along with the timeline.

Here's where most service disintegrates

It's up to you to ensure the issue's been resolved. You own the problem even if you've passed it on. Remember, unless you're perfect, your organization will make mistakes. How you handle them exposes your abilities and intent - for better or worse.

Chapter 26

Dangers of Couponing

A while ago, I called one of the national pizza chains to have a pizza delivered. They asked for my phone number and I heard the person working on her keyboard. I order the pizza and then she asks me, "Do you have any coupons today?" Since I didn't, I feel like everybody else in the world is paying less money for that pizza than me, which makes me feel real "special."

That's one of the dangers of offering special discounts via the mass media to only a segment of your marketplace. You end up alienating

INSTEAD OF COUPONING CONSIDER A CROSS PROMOTION LIKE THIS SUCCESSFUL ONE BETWEEN MOE'S SOUTHWEST GRILL AND STAPLES.

some customers because they were first informed of the special pricing but then denied it because they didn't have the coupon.

While this can be very helpful in generating short-term sales, it can be a problem for you down the road. If you should continue to

62

offer deals for any protracted length of time, the danger is that you'll condition your customers to wait for the deal before they will buy from you. Many of our clients have expressed concerns about shrinking profit margins as a result of a loss of pricing credibility. Coupons and sales are effective. When you use any type of off-price tactics be sure you protect your price credibility in the process. One way to protect your price credibility and still attract buying customers is to use a cross promotion.

•. **Transfer Responsibility of the Discount**. When you run a coupon, the consumer knows you paid money to offer a deal on your product or service. However, if you were able to get another organization to distribute your offer to its customers or members on your behalf, it helps to transfer the responsibility of that offer to your cross promotion partner. Make sure on your promotional piece you say, "compliments of" the organization handing them out.

Free Advertising

Another advantage of this cross promotion approach is that you get your advertising piece distributed to your customer, free. This is a great way to supplement your existing advertising budget without additional cost. Even the actual printed piece doesn't have to be that expensive. Since it is being handed out at the register with a purchase or as a bag stuffer, you don't need full-color to get the customer's attention like you would with a direct mail campaign.

Targeted

Another advantage is the ability to target types of customers you want by demographics. In the example given, both the grocery store and the appliance store wanted to reach the same target audience. It made sense for them to promote each other.

Geographic

Most retail businesses get their customers within a certain area surrounding their business, perhaps two to five miles. So, if you want to focus your efforts to a certain part of the city, you simply set up a cross promotion with a partner located in the area you want the concentration. This also comes into play when you have multiple locations in a market but want to get more aggressive with one of them.

Chapter 27

Talking Your Way To The Top

There is perhaps no greater skill that can help you build your career or business than effective public speaking. Whether you're speaking to a small committee of ten decision makers or an arena filled with 10,000 future leaders, knowing how to persuasively present your point of view can make the difference between merely surviving or thriving in a vastly competitive environment.

Goals Of Public Speaking

No matter what you do for a vocation or avocation, public speaking can be a valuable tool for increasing the level of your success. There are many advantages in becoming an effective public speaker to present your message. Perhaps four of the most obvious, in ascending order of success level, would include: Awareness, Understanding, Impact, and Action.

Awareness

Whether you're presenting information on a service, product, or a point of view, public speaking provides you a medium to expose your audiences to the advantages of what you have to offer. Awareness, from a marketing point of view, is the first level of starting to achieve your goals through public speaking. Awareness in this respect means a superficial impression, notion or perception about your message.

Understanding

Practically any speech will help create some degree of awareness for the message but to get a better result from your effort you want the audience go beyond a superficial awareness. You want them to understand your message. To do this, gear that speech to address the needs and wants of your audience. Understanding here means a greater comprehension of your message. To achieve a greater understanding you need to develop and deliver that message with a great skill. The more effective you are in your presentation skills, the greater the chances that your audience comprehends and remembers the key points of your message.

Impact

Just because your audience members understand your points, doesn't necessarily mean that they agree with your message. To persuade using public speaking you must impact your audience. At this level, you've not only helped your audience members remember your key points, but you've caused them, through your persuasive style and message to actually "buy into" your message. You want your combined message and style to reach them on an emotional level.

Action

The ultimate result for a public speaker is to combine both the message and the presentation style so effectively that it causes members of your audience to take a suggested course of action. This is certainly the most difficult result to obtain from a speech but generally the ultimate goal a speaker has in mind.

The rewards of mastering your public speaking ability go beyond giving that speech and reaching that particular audience.

Increased Credibility

Public speaking is a form of persuasive communication that literally puts you on a pedestal. Since the vast majority of people in your audiences are scared to death to speak in front of a group, the audience is likely to admire your passion and talent for speaking. The assumption by your audience might be that "if you're speaking on the subject, you must be an expert." You will prove or disprove this assumption by presenting your speech, but in most cases your audiences will give you the benefit of the doubt.

Chapter 28

Handling A PR Crisis

Recently we were helping promote one of our seminars. We had the support of the local Chamber of Commerce in that city who provided us their membership e-mail list so we could offer a special "member to member" discount to the Chamber members. Unfortunately, what started out as an economical marketing program turned into a marketing nightmare.

We first noticed a problem that evening when we started getting "mailer demons" every few seconds. Within an hour there were over 500 returned emails to our address. Apparently, there was a virus and a hacker that caused our e-mail to be replicated repeatedly to everyone on the list. Not only was our e-mail account getting overloaded, so were the other 2000 people on that list. Each one of them thought we were sending those emails. There were some angry people, to say the least.

This is a classic marketing crisis situation. The problem was totally out of our control, yet we were getting all the negative PR. So we immediately went into crisis mode:

Identify the problem

In our case the problem was an e-mail message masquerading as if it came from us and it was being transmitted over and over, literally hundreds of times to each of the individual's e-mail boxes.

Develop a response

We started getting phone calls right away. Since the e-mail originally went out on a Friday night, we actually got calls at our home on Saturday. To deal with the issue, we scripted our response. First, we let them know that we were aware of the problem. Second, we apologize for the inconvenience. It's just as big an inconvenience for us as you. Third, we asked them to please understand that these emails were not coming from us. Fourth, we were doing everything we could to solve the problem.

We made sure that our staff followed that format. Plus, no matter the tone of the caller, they were to be pleasant and apologetic. Of the many dozens of calls we received, the vast majority of the people, once we explained the situation, understood it and were empathetic. We also changed the outbound message of our voice mail to explain the problem. Once the inbound calls slowed down to a trickle, we changed the outbound message back to the original message.

Fix the problem

The next step was to try to fix the problem, if it's fixable. We called our internet provider who started an investigation for us. We also contacted our IT provider to see if they could figure anything out. Next we contacted the Chamber. They, too received many phone calls. We explained the situation to them and, like everyone else, were understanding. They offered to send out a brief article explaining the situation in their weekly newsletter.

The last step was to make sure it never happens again. In our case that means that we will be very careful when doing bulk e-mails and only use a reputable service to do them for us instead of internally.

When faced with such a PR crisis, we suggest to always attack the problem head on. Don't hide or shuck responsibility. At the same time, take a brief period of time to outline your response. By dealing with the issues and allowing irate customers to vent, you'll do much to minimize the damage.

Chapter 29

Suggestive Selling Increases Profits At Very Little Cost

Suggest-selling is a simple and inexpensive marketing technique used at the time of a purchase to increase sales and profitability. It is often relatively easy to add 10-20 percent to an existing sale or get an existing customer to buy just one more item or perhaps a larger version of a given item. One technique that we suggest business people try is to properly suggest the most profitable version of the item being ordered.

For example, in a restaurant, when a customer orders a soft drink or other items that come in several sizes, most servers ask, "what size?" Instead of asking the customer which size item he or she wants, respond with, "Is large okay?" By suggesting the most profitable option, you are likely to increase the number of large items sold. That translates into additional profits without any additional marketing dollars being spent.

Another way to increase your average transaction is suggesting an additional complimentary item. Oftentimes this can add another 20-30 percent more to the transaction. We've used this approach when offering one of our audio albums in a direct response campaign. The special offer allowed them to buy an $80 album for only $49. When they called into to buy the album, we also offered them an additional single CD of a live speech on a similar subject. They could add this bonus CD to their order for only $9.95. We found that half of the call in orders also agreed to pay the additional $9.95 for the CD. That resulted in increasing the average transaction by $4.97, or a little more than 10 percent.

The key to implementing this add-on strategy is to first identify those products or services that you can easily use to add-on to a sale. The add-on item needs to have a higher profit margin, be easily sold and add value of between 10 and 20 percent of the main product or services you sell.

The next thing to keep in mind is the timing of offering the add-on product or service. Do this just after you've confirmed the main sale. After you've gotten the commitment from your customer or client, make your add-on suggestion. It usually goes something like this, "By the way, many of our customers like to have the benefit of our (insert name of item) which allows you to get even more value from the (insert name of item just sold). It's only (insert price) more. Would you like me to toss that in for you?" Notice the low-key presentation. You want to make it sound like you just thought of this extra thing.

Lastly, as you start working with your add-on program, be sure to track your results. Through trial and error, you'll be able to determine the best item and price-point for your add-on program. Once you do, continue to fine-tune that offering to see if it's possible to improve it further. Test the results by raising or lowering the price of the add-on slightly. Also, experiment with other add-on items. Try to uncover if it is possible to substitute your current successful add-on item with another one that is more profitable at the same price-point.

Chapter 30

A Special Mailing

Most, so called, "junk mail" ends up in the trash. Yet, enough bulk mailings are successful so we continue to get tons of the stuff every day. We discovered a mailing program that gave us very good results. The odd thing was, that we had used this same exact approach many years ago. It was successful then but we stopped using it until recently.

A number of years ago, Prentice Hall called me and told me they were taking my very first book, *Streetfighting: Low Cost Marketing for Your Business,* out of print. At the time it was my only book. (Since then we've published 11 books). I thought this was going to be a disaster, yet it turned out to be the biggest blessing in disguise.

They informed me that I could buy the "remainders." This is their remaining inventory. At the time, I was buying the book for about $10 each which was a 50% discount on the retail price. They told me they would sell them to me for $1.29 each! I asked how many they had. The answer was 3,206. I took them all.

Several weeks later, a truck shows up at my office with 75 cases of books. I had them put in the basement of my apartment at that time. Since I had so many copies of the book in stock, I started thinking of ways to leverage that inventory. One way was to use them as a promotional tool. At $1.29, it was cheaper than some four-color brochures. I created a list of 300 companies I wanted to do business with. I then send out five autographed books a day to companies on that list, along with a cover letter and brochure.

I figured they would never throw away a book. I was right. I started getting calls. Some hired us for speaking and consulting and others just ordered quantities of the book. Within a couple of years the entire inventory was gone and I had to reorder the books from the printer.

Not too long ago, we took delivery of a new order of books. So, we took a page from our company's history and started mailing autographed hard cover books to companies on our hit list. Our sales team then followed up. But even before the first follow up call was made, we got an inbound call which lead to a sizable consulting contract. Here are some suggestions on how to make this work for you:

Work from a higher quality list. First, determine what item you can mail that your prospects will find valuable. Don't just send junk mail to the masses. Rather, get a more qualified list and send something that will get their attention. You are much better off working from a smaller list that has been fine-tuned than to just mail tons of stuff out and hope for the best.

We even have our sales people call the list first and pre-qualify it. We want to get the name of the decision maker and confirm that the address is correct. Since we're sending out a package that had a retail value of over $35, we wanted to make sure it was going to end up in the right hands.

Pick a high value item. What do you have that is a high perceived value, yet the actual cost is very little? Furthermore, that item should represent or demonstrate your product or service. You may not have a book to send but you might have an item that would get a lot of attention.

Follow up. Don't count on the mailer to get you the results by itself. If you get inbound calls that's great, but plan on following up. That means you only want to send out as many pieces as your staff has time to conduct follow up phone calls. You may want to send out your pieces in waves. If you plan to send out 500 pieces, perhaps you send out 25 pieces a day over 20 days. This gives you more time to do the follow up phone calls.

Chapter 31

Guerrilla Publicity - The Dos and Don'ts of Media Follow-up

The way you handle the media is the key to achieving desired success. They are finicky. Aim for the headlines, Jill Lublin has the inside scoop on what makes the media smile and what makes them cringe.

15 things the media hates/15 things the media loves:

1. Not take "no" for an answer. . . . . 1. News
2. Long news releases. . . . . 2. Brevity, Be Clear
3. Lying, hype, an d misrepresentations. . . . . 3. Knowing targets
4. Lack of Preparation. . . . . 4. Relationships
5. Small Talk. . . . . 5. Preparation
6. Overkill. . . . . 6. Broad appeal
7. No repeated cold calling. 7.Ties
8. Freebies. . . . . 8. Experience
9. Name dropping. . . . . 9. Visualization
10. Lack of focus. . . . . 10. Celebrity tie-ins
11. Confirmation calls. . . . . 11. Prompt response
12. Gimmicks. . . . . .12. Courtesy
13. Not following up requests. . . . . .13. Visual aids

14. Same ideas. . . . . 14. No road blocks
15. Getting upset. . . . . 15. A pleasant attitude

Jill Lublin is a public relations / marketing consultant and CEO of the public relations consultancy, Promising Promotion, located in Novato, California. She speaks nationally and teaches powerful and practical public relations techniques that anyone can use. Jill is also the Co-Founder of the company, Good News Media, and host of the nationally syndicated radio show, "Do the Dream" She is also the author the national best selling book, Guerrilla Publicity (Adams Media), part of the Jay Levinson Guerrilla Marketing Series. Jill Lublin can be reached at (415) 883-5455 or by e-mail info@promisingpromotion.com

Chapter 32

A Competitive Exit Strategy Helps Bring In Old Customers

When one or more of your competitors goes out of business, dramatically increase your business with a "competitive exit" program. Here are a few tactics that businesses have used successfully:

Get The Old Phone Number

If a competitor of yours has closed their doors in the last several years, (and did not sell it someone else), consider getting their old phone number. To see if that number is available, call it. If you get a phone company generated recording, your next step is to call your local service provider to see if they can get you that number. Joe, of Home Town Appliance did this and told us it cost them less than $30 a month. The old number is simply forwarded to their own number. In the first month, they noticed an average increase in their inbound calls of 15 percent. The reason for this new business is that the old competitor still has an address and phone sticker out with that phone number and perhaps even internet search engines, webite or landing pages and possibly even a Yellow Pages ad still being used.

Ask For The Referral

If the old number is currently being used by a noncompetitive business or person, you can offer to buy the number from them for a year or so. Pay for the extra phone line so that the number can be forwarded to your business. If they don't want to do that, you might inform them that they'll probably be getting calls for your type of business. Tell them that you would appreciate if they would give your number when they get those wrong numbers. Then offer to buy them a nice dinner or something for their effort. Sometimes these arrangements can be made directly with the receptionist.

If there is a delay because the number has not been released yet, you can do what Bob in Cincinnati did for his sewing machine dealership. He called the former owner and offered him $100 to call the phone company on his behalf, for an intercept message. This way when a customer called the old number, instead of hearing that it was disconnected, the customer hears that the number has been changed. The new number in the message is Bob's.

Buy The Customer List

A former competitor's mailing list can be a very valuable asset for someone still in the business. Offer to buy the list. Even if the list is a little out of date, it still could provide you with more new customers. Do a series of mailings to that list. Make sure the first mailing is first class so that you can get the returns of the bad addresses and can clean it up for future mailings.

Put Up A Banner

The banner says something like, this company is out of business but if you're looking for someone to take care of your needs, call our number. This is the approach a tire dealer outside of Denver used when his competitor vacated a building across the street. He got permission from the landlord, for a small fee, to put up a banner for a few months with his address and phone under the condition that he honor all their tire warranties.

Mirror Their Advertising

If the competitor ran ad consistently over the years, run your ad in the same place and at the same times. Have the style of your ad similar to the old competitor's but with your information.

Chapter 33

Voice Mail That Gets Calls Returned

"HELLO, MR. SMITH? THIS IS C.J. SLUTSKY..."

Voice mail is a nightmare for reaching decision makers, unless you have an approach that's a dream come true. When I get voice mail, my first tactic is to leave a message. I make it clear, to the point and with very few details. I also say my phone number very slowly and then repeat it to make it easy to jot it down. But if nothing I try works, then I have to get a little creative. That's when I use a simple idea that was taught to me by my friend, Orval Ray Wilson, the coauthor of *Guerilla Telephone Selling*. I get my son, C.J. on the phone to leave the message for me. He'll say, "Mr. Smith? This is C.J. Slutsky. My Dad, Jeff Slutsky's been trying to get a hold of you for a while. And he said that he would take me to Disney World just as soon as you return his call." Well, do you think it worked? So far this year alone I owe my son 14 trips to Disney.

Chapter 34

Hire the best employees, and make sure you retain them

(Part 1 of 4)

You have spent a great deal of time, money and effort recruiting employees for your company. You want to make sure the people you have spent so much time *getting* to your organization; *stay*. Marc Ankerman, business professor at *The* Ohio State University and former Director of Learning and Development at Express (a division of Limited Inc.) identifies 5 ways to help you retain your employees longer.

Do your homework

Take the time to research what it is like for a new person who joins your company. Do they get greeted when they come in the door? Does someone take them to lunch on the first day? Are their desk, phone, computer and general workplace ready for them during their first week on the new job? Have focus groups ask employees what it was like for them on their first day. Find out all you can from the employees who are still with your company: they understand retention!

Experience the orientation

Most companies have some form of orientation. Even if it is a short meeting with Human Resources, you should try to spend time looking at the material which is given to new employees. Find the time to sit through an orientation yourself. Doing an audit will provide you with firsthand knowledge of the questions and initial perception, as well as give you a chance to see what information (both correct and incorrect) is given to newcomers to your organization.

Create an atmosphere of learning

Make sure you give the new hire a chance to learn about the culture, the environment and even the most mundane parts of the building in which they work. Orientation is just that: Orientating the new employees to their surroundings, their new work environment, and the culture of the workplace. By providing this information during the first week, the employees can focus on their changes in a productive manner.

Create an on-boarding program

On-boarding is a long term program, which includes learning, experiences, interaction with senior management, and a variety of other training and experiential programs throughout the first year of the new employees' time with the company. The one year on-boarding program allows your new employee to experience a complete business cycle of your company. On-boarding, through a set of activities, provides the employee with the skills and information needed to get assimilated quickly and correctly with their new company.

Redesign and update often

As you develop and re-develop the orientation or larger on-boarding program, remember that it needs constant tweaking. It might be a new business, or process, or client you have added which needs to be included in an action item for your new employee. Be aware of changes to the executive team or leadership group, which may mandate changes to your programs. It is easy to update the program if you have built in learning modules, which can grow and change. The best course of action is to make sure you evaluate after each session, taking the feedback from participants seriously, as they are your next best clients in the retention of great employees.

SMART MARKETING ACTION PLAN

- Do your homework, and find out about the current programs you have at work.
- Experience the orientation, by making time to sit in on the program and see what it is like for a new employee.
- Create an atmosphere where every experience is a learning experience.
- Create an on-boarding program.
- Re-design and update the program as changes in your business occur.

For info: http://www.case-chosencandidates.com

Chapter 35

Motivational Movie Quotes For Business

Fire up your troops each morning with a motivational movie quote. Jeff and coauthor, Larry Winget, have released a new book entitled, *From The Big Screen To The Real World*. It divides their favorite motivational quotes form the movies into 17 different topics. Here are some samples:

Life.

"You can do anything with your life that you want to" — *Arthur*, Sir John Gielgud (Hobson)

"What we do in life, echoes in eternity." — *Gladiator*, Russell Crowe. (Maximus Decimus Meridius)

Success.

"You don't need a patch on your arm to have honor." — *A Few Good Men,* Tom Cruise (Lt. Kaffee)

"The road to genius is paved with fumble-footing and bumbling. Anyone who falls flat on his face is at least moving in the right direction…forward. And the fellow who makes the most mistakes may be the one who will save the neck of the whole world someday." — *Son Of Flubber*, Fred Macmurray (Ned Brainard)

Goals.

"You gotta see yourself making it." — *An Officer And A Gentleman*, Debra Winger

Money.

"Never knew how poor I was until I started making money."
Wall Street, Michael Douglas, (Gordon Gekko)

Love.

"Real loss is only possible when you love something more than you love yourself." — *Good Will Hunting*, Robin Williams (Sean McGuire)

"A bird may love a fish, but where would they build a home together?" — Fiddler on the Roof, Topel (Tevye)

Communication.

"It doesn't matter what I believe. It only matters what I can prove." — *A Few Good Men*, Tom Cruise, (Lt. Kaffee)

Customer Service.

"Was here earlier. I wanted that dress. You threw me out. Big mistake, huge!!" (Showing bags full of expensive purchases) — *Pretty Woman*, Julia Roberts (after asking if she worked on commission)

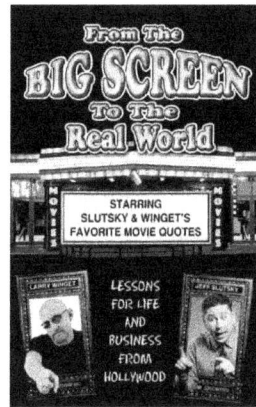

Leadership.

"I am the commander in chief, and I decide when we go to war!" — *Thirteen Days*, Bruce Greenwood (President John F. Kennedy)

"It's not about the details. It's about the big picture." — *Ed Wood*, Johnny Depp (Ed Wood)

Management.

"Rommel…I Read Your Book!" —*Patton*, George C. Scott (Gen. Patton)

"I can't fix it if I don't know what's broke." — *Heartbreak Ridge*, Clint Eastwood (Gunnery Sgt. Thomas Highway)

"We make sacred pact. I promise teach karate to you, you promise learn. I say, you do, no questions."— *The Karate Kid*, Pat Morita (Mr. Miyagi)

Negotiations..

"Well, you get what you settle for." —*Thelma And Louise*, Susan Sarandon (Louise)

Change

"I'll change; I'll change. I've learned that I have the strength to change." — *The Godfather, Part II,* Al Pacino (Michael Corleone)

"Life goes on, even for those of us who are divorced, broke, and sloppy." — *The Odd Couple*, Walter Mathau (Oscar Madison)

"Just 'cause I rock doesn't mean I'm made of stone." — *Me, Myself and Irene*, Jim Carey.

"You never open your mouth until you know what the shot is." — *Glengarry Glen Ross*, Al Pacino to Kevin Spacey

SMART MARKETING ACTION PLAN

- Determine the topic you wish to discuss at your next staff meeting.
- Find an appropriate movie quote that reinforces the theme of the meeting.
- Share the quote with the group.
- If the quote is relevant only in the context of the movie, be sure to explain the scene and circumstances.
- As the group how this quote applies to your situation.

Chapter 36

Pizza Promotions Sells Some Pie

A pizza shop had an opportunity to work with Marc Slutsky, Vice President of Street Fighter Marketing. Utilizing his Street Fighter ideas and techniques this pizza shop had an opportunity to provide a valuable service for their community.

The owner heard about a local family whose house burned down. They lost practically everything. "We wanted to raise money for this family so we decided to have a benefit weekend for them."

The owner approached the family to arrange the event. The family would receive, half of the pizza sales generated, over what they normally sell from Thursday through Saturday. However, it was up to the family and their friends to promote the event. By putting forth a major promotional effort, the family could potentially raise a great deal of money to help them get back on their feet. And they did. They passed out flyers and put up posters in every single business in their strip center where they were located, except Domino's!

The results were phenomenal. The event was a huge success for both the family and the pizza shop. $1300 was raised for the family and the business doubled sales and their customer count during the event.

- Seventy percent were new customers.
- There was TV exposure on the CBS, ABC and Fox affiliates

newscasts plus several articles in two suburban newspapers.

- Dozens of area businesses promoted the event in their stores, and donated printing of posters, flyers and banners.
- The out of pocket expense was a mere $10. (for the permit to put up the promotional banner, which of course, was donated).

Chapter 37

Using Postcards Gets More Customers

Most mail advertising ends in the trash. But, a postcard with the right message can increase your readership dramatically. Here are several "Street Fighter" examples of a low cost, high impact mailing campaign:

While in Las Vegas for her annual quick printer's convention, the owner of a print shop in Solon, Ohio bought 400 picture postcards from the MGM Grand. She brought them back to her shop and had her kids hand address them with the names of 400 businesses who were not her customers. The message on the back of the postcard read, "Don't gamble with your printing needs. Bring this postcard in for a 10% savings on your first printing order." She received 100 redemptions! That's a 25% return. The reason? It didn't look like junk mail. If you got a picture postcard from Vegas, you'd probably ask yourself, "who do I know in Vegas and how much did they win?" You then turn it over to see who it was from and the headline of, "Don't Gamble With Your (insert the name of your service)," gets to you see and remember the offer. Plus, you mail at the postcard rate instead of regular first class which saves you some postage.

While in Nashville addressing a group of real estate agents from all over the US, I told this story then gave them the assignment to find picture postcards. Then they were to get a list of 25 potential clients, create a headline that tied into the picture on the postcard and mail them from Nashville. One creative group found postcards with horses running through a pasture. Their headline: "Don't horse around when you want to sell your home fast."

My favorite Street Fighter type postcard mailer was done by a realtor in Columbus, Ohio. This real estate agent mailed a simple postcard to several hundreds homes. He was offering a free home warranty if you listed with him. But, the postcard was boring. It was black ink on grey card stock and didn't look particularly appealing. As expected, 100 percent of his mailing was trashed. A week later those same homes receive an envelope from the same guy. Inside the envelope was the same post card that had been crumpled up and then flattened. Attached to the crumpled postcard was a yellow sticky note that read, "Please don't throw this out again! This is important." People must have been saying to themselves, "Is this guy going through the trash? He must really know the neighborhood. We gotta give him a call!"

Another clever use of an inexpensive postcard mailing was done by a Scuba store in San Francisco. They promoted a diving trip to Maui. Many of his customers inquired about the trip but only a third, as expected, actually signed up for it. The store owner took the list of people who couldn't make it this time. From Maui, he mailed picture postcards and a wrote a brief message of what a wonderful time they were having. What a great way to build up strong interest for future trips. Also, while there had have each of his participants three postcards with postage and asked them to write a "wish your were here" message to their scuba friends back home. It was a great way to generate referral business. That's how a "Streetfighter" runs a business!

Greeting Cards

Help Increase Customer Loyalty: There's many advantages of using greeting cards to capture the attention of your hot prospects and build loyalty with your existing customers and clients:
- They're relatively cheap.
- They're readily available at any card shop and many other stores.

- They're high quality printed pieces.
- They're available in great variety.
- And, they almost always get opened and read.

In order to make an impact, you want to use these greeting cards in unusual ways.

Giving Thanks For Their Business

Scott Friedman, a professional speaker based in Denver,.Colorado, told us, "I send out Thanksgiving cards in November instead of Christmas and Hanukkah cards in December. All of my clients get tons of cards in late December, but they usually get only one Thanksgiving card a month earlier. And they remember my card more than all of the others."

Hair Today For Tomorrow

A local hair stylist used greeting cards when he switched salons. After relocating from the northern part of the city to a new salon just south of Downtown, he was disappointed to find that 18 customers didn't make the switch. Each month he would send a different greeting card and simply write the message, "I miss you." One month he only mailed his business card with that same message on the back. Over the following twelve months, all 18 returned to his styling chair.

When You Really Love Their Business, Let Them Know It. Valentine's Day and to a lesser degree, Sweetest Day are two opportunities to share your feelings with your customers and clients. The card should be on the lighter side. Be sure to write a business response on the inside of the card like, "We love doing business with you." or "For a sweetheart of a deal, give me a call . . ." It's best to have the card signed by several key people in your organization or sign it as your business. (You don't want to give anyone the wrong impression.)

Get Well Soon

Another idea is to have a small inventory of special greeting cards that you can use as the need arises. This would include Condolences,

Get Well Soon, Congratulations, Happy Birthday, Happy Anniversary (which can be used for Wedding Anniversaries or the anniversary of employment). Warning: If you're planning to use a wedding anniversary card for a client you haven't been in touch with for a while, it's a good idea to make sure that person is still married. It could be really embarrassing if you sent an anniversary card when you should have sent a condolence card or one of congratulations.

You're The Boss.

Just when we finally got used to Sweetest Day, they came out with Boss's; Day. Well, fortunately we don't have to worry about that one. But there is an opportunity. Think of the impact you would make sending a Boss's Day card to some of your key customers or clients with the message, "You're The Boss."

Chapter 38

Business Cards Can Connect You To More Customers

You can easily turn a simple, inexpensive business card into a powerful marketing too! All you have to do, two to three times a day, is hand out your card to someone who is not your customer or client. Start with people you already come in contact with. When you're running errands, for example, you're likely to come in contact with the waiter at the local restaurant, the grocery store clerk, hair stylist, your mail carrier, the dry cleaner clerk, the check out person at the discount store, and even the police officer giving you a warning to slow down. The list is endless. Simply hand them your business card then introduce yourself and invite them to become your customers or client.

Free Cup of Coffee Creates New Customers.

Barbara is the manager of a convenience store in Parkersburg, West Virginia. During an eleven week period, she passed out 200 of her business cards to people she did not recognize as being her customers. On the back of her business card she would write "free regular soft drink or coffee" and signed it. Then she would tell them that when they come into her convenience store, the soft drink was on her. Of the

200 she passed out, 51 came in to redeem her offer. That's over a 25 percent return. Obviously most of those who came in and redeemed that card, bought other things. Plus, many of those customers came back for more visits.

Hind Sight Promotion

A very successful stock broker on the East Coast used a different version of business card distribution according to Murray Raphael, author of *The Great Brain Robbery*. While commuting to work, this stock broker would have to pay several tolls. Before he would pay his tolls, he would first look in his rear view mirror. If he would see an upscale car, he not only would pay his toll but also pay the toll of the person in the luxury car behind him. He then asked the toll booth attendant to hand his business card to the person in the car behind him after writing a brief note on the back of the card. The note read, "If you think this is an interesting way of getting your attention, think of all the things I could do for your financial portfolio." He got many new clients off of a simple 90¢ toll and a clever use of his business card.

Increase the average purchase to improve the bottom line: Suggest-selling is a simple and inexpensive marketing technique used at the time of a purchase to increase sales and profitability. It is often relatively easy to add 10-20% more to an existing sale or get an existing customer to buy just one more item.

Consider the restaurant that despite having really great banana cream pie had very weak dessert sales. To motivate his wait staff to suggest dessert more aggressively, he ran a contest. For one month, the server who would sell the most banana cream pies would win . . . one banana cream pie. And they would get to throw it in the owner's face! You never saw such a motivated crew in your life. Just by getting them to suggest dessert, the restaurant's dessert sales increased nearly 50% during the contest.

An ice cream manufacturer in Canada wanted to promote its product more aggressively through a convenience store chain. They offered to provide to the chain a contest enticing their employees to suggest-sell the ice cream bars at the cash register during a purchase. It was suggested that the ice cream company use a mystery shopper approach where each store would be visited several times during the month. If the employee would suggest-sell an ice cream bar to the mystery shopper, that employee was handed a $50 bill on the spot. If they failed, they were handed a printed note telling them they just lost $50 but they may get another chance. A contest like this creates excitement for employees and as soon as someone wins some cash, the word spreads.

Suggest-selling doesn't have to be limited to food items or contests. A good example from a service business is the approach we use in our own business. Once a client has booked one of us for a sales or marketing seminar for a meeting or convention, our sales people offer to sell copies of our book, Street Fighter Marketing, in quantity for the attendees. When books are purchased as an "add-on" to a speaking contract, the client gets them for less then half of the retail price. This happens about one-third of the time and generally adds about another 50% to that sale. Those clients get a great price for the books, their attendees walk away with something tangible in their hands from the seminar and we increase our sales.

Fish Bowl Promotions

Knowing who your customers are allows you to update your customer base and grow your business. Many businesses attempt to acquire a customer list, but fail to take full advantage of that list once they get it.

One of the easiest ways to find out who your customers are is offering a business card drawing when they visit your store. Put a fishbowl on your counter, and anybody who comes into your place of business can place their business card in there for a chance to win a prize. Patrick, the general manager of a texmex restaurant in Maumee, Ohio, has been using the fishbowl for several years. He says."The fishbowl is instrumental in building our data base which allowed us to increase our sales through direct mail."

The following process can increase your chance of collecting the cards and take full advantage of the names you collect.

- **Have an attractive bowl** - Too many companies use a cardboard box or a cheap piece of plastic as a means to collect the cards. Spend a few dollars and find a bowl that will look good on your counter.

- **Create a professional looking sign** - To draw attention to your fishbowl create a sign which explains what prize the customer will win by having his business card picked from the fishbowl.
- **Train your employees** - Make sure your employees are trained to know how to respond to your customers and remind them to drop their business card in the fish bowl. That will ensure more of your customers participate in the drawing. Be sure to keep it out in the open so the customer can see it and it becomes a constant reminder to your employee to get more participation.
- **Incorporate your data base** - When the fishbowl starts to fill up, take the names and add them to your data base. Over a period of time your data base of names will grow to a substantial number.
- **Keep in contact** - Now that you have a growing list of names, it is critical to keep in contact with everyone in your data base. This allows you to remind your customers about you, and perhaps keep them away from your competitors. Also, make sure you are consistent in keeping in contact. Try to do it at lease once a quarter. This can be accomplished by a direct mail piece, phone call or a newsletter.
- **Special offer** - When you make contact with people in your data base, have some kind of special offer for that customer to visit your store in the near future. Remember, it is less expensive to get a regular customer to buy from you again, then it is to find a new customer.
- **Mix it up** - Alternate mailings with emails, if you have permission to use their e-mail address. But, don't make phone calls. That will only annoy your customers.

Chapter 39

Biz Blunders: Successful business people learn from their mistakes

Making mistakes from taking risks is part of the educational process for any successful business person. The more mistakes you make, the more you can potentially learn, provided you don't keep making the same mistakes over again. For now, let's learn from other people's mistakes:

Ovary Oops!

When the client returns to the Vet to pick up his AKC registered Champion show dog, he notices that his bill seems awfully high for a bath and spray. So he mentioned that he felt it seemed pretty pricey to the tune of $100, just to get his dog clean and flea free. That's when he discovered that he was being billed for a *bath and spay*. The lawsuit that followed basically rendered the Vet financially neutered. We don't know if they every got rid of the fleas. Lesson: Give your customers what they want.

Sweet Surprise

We were recently told of a new kosher style deli that was having problems with their young servers because they just weren't familiar with the product line. It seems they couldn't tell the difference between corned beef and a corn dog. One customer orders a Reuben sandwich on challah. Challah (pronounced *cha'*-la, where the "ch" is a guttural) is traditional Jewish, braided bread. When his ordered arrived he was surprised to see that they put his sandwich on halvah, (pronounced *chal'*-vah') which is a very sweet, candy-like desert. Lesson: Before you let your employees serve your customers or clients, make sure they understand the products and services you offer.

Chicken Feed

Making mistakes in business is part of doing business. The key is to learn from those experiences. We've had our share of Biz Blunders over the years. Marc was the volunteer chairperson for an ad-hoc committee of a non profit organization. The problem was that he couldn't get his committee members to attend the meetings and this was causing his time involvement to be much greater than he anticipated. He had only one scheduled meeting left. He wanted to insure that a quorum would be present so they could vote on their final recommendation and then he'd be free of this task once and for all.

To motivate his committee members to attend, he mailed out a flier that promised them a free chicken dinner at the end of the meeting. Everyone showed up. After the vote he treated them to their free chicken dinner: little packets of dried corn! Lesson: don't do this.

The Key

In a similar situation, when the committee chair knew he was going to have a hard time getting all his members to show up to their meeting, he sent each one a note that said, "I'm going to be a little late to the meeting. Please open up for me." He included a key with the note which he got from a locksmith. The keys didn't open anything but made a great prop. Everyone showed up on time.

Insensitive Situation

Then there was the fast food franchise owner who was so proud of his new braille menu, that he had it laminated. Lesson: Use a little common sense.

Chapter 40

Your Best Credential. Certification!

Part 2 of 4

In the hiring world, it is not only whom you know, but also what credentials you have. Marc Ankerman, business professor at *The* Ohio State University and former Director of Learning and Development at Express (a division of Limited Inc.),has seen how certification assists candidates in the interviewing process and inevitably landing the jobs of their dreams.

In the training and development arena, Certification is measurement, validation, and the "meat" of good training. It is simply not enough to have exposure to learning by taking a course or seminar. It is in the ability to measure what you have learned, through testing (or certification) that indicates you have achieved competence.

It is not enough to have good stories about projects and activities you have worked on during your employment. Today's employers want to be able to know that the training you have received is valid and comes from a reputable source.

A good example of this is the current feeling by many employers that the interview process does not provide enough qualified information.

Many employers feel that they cannot just take the word of the applicant anymore, but they have to "test" to make sure the skills are real and applicable. The tests are costly and often times do not tell the full picture. Some applicants may have the skill or knowledge, but lack the ability to pass the new employers testing vehicle and do not get the job. The one exception to this however, is certification. If, for example, an applicant tells you that they are proficient in Microsoft Word, you are not sure if that means they can type, or maneuver through the process, or create a full document. If they are certified in that piece of software, you know their abilities and their skill level and are more assured of their competence in the skill.

Certification serves as a tool, not only for the employer (in knowing the achievement level of the skill), but also for the applicant. The more certifications you have the easier it is for the hiring manager to know what you can and cannot do. It is one of the reasons ATS partnered with SmartPursuit (www.smartpursuit.com). ATS helped to create the certification process for a series of courses, which teach skills and concepts in a variety of functional areas. The key is that "certification" means that the student in this case, has been able to take the information and apply the knowledge via a testing vehicle. It is more than just sitting through the class or viewing the information. The SmartPursuit series provides credible knowledge and learning to assist in a wide variety of skills and abilities. The Certification (and in this case testing) helps provide the user with the credentials to support the experiences and learning, which they have received.

We know that a SmartPursuit Certification on a resume means that the learner has knowledge and abilities. The hiring manager can rest assured that the new employee has already been tested and certified in the areas of achievement. It saves time for the hiring managers, gives credibility for the end-user and provides a great forum for experiences the applicant can share with a prospective employer.

More Smart Marketing Action Plan:

- As an employer, use certifications as a way to document the skill sets a prospective employee posts on a resume
- As a potential employee, use certifications to prove your abilities in those specific skill sets.
- Use certifications as a way to improve your skill sets and make yourself more attractive to a potential job.

For info: http://www.case-chosencandidates.com

Chapter 41

Courting Customers For Long-Term Success

As a business owner, you're motivated to find new customers because you see an immediate payoff in sales and profits. Yet, what you do for your customers after the sale has even more impact on your long-term success.

Studies by Harvard University and others show it costs five times as much to win new customers as to keep existing customers engaged with your business. Savvy businesses put building relationships with customers at the top of their priority list.

Cheryl, a communications manager with Greencrest, a Columbus-based marketing, advertising and public relations agency, says that the customer relationship life cycle is like any other relationship. It begins in the courtship phase. She gives these tips for forming lasting, committed relationships with your customers.

Start off by wowing new customers

You are inspired to enter a relationship because your partner makes you feel special and appreciated. Impress your new customers by delivering more than they expect. Include a free sample of a related product. Upgrade to overnight delivery at no charge. Make sure your customers aren't just satisfied — they are delighted!

Follow up

A first sale is like a first date. Make a follow-up call to make sure the customer was pleased and to offer complementary products or services. Send a thank-you card with a discount offer on future orders. Keep the love alive..

Get feedback

Maintaining any relationship requires open, honest communication to build trust and respect. Ask your customers about their experience with your company. Were all their expectations met? If not, find out why, and make sure it doesn't happen again. Typical businesses lose half their customers in fewer than five years, but few customers leave when they are truly receiving superior value.

Don't take your customer for granted. If feeling ignored or unappreciated, one partner will leave a relationship as soon as someone better comes along. You can't assume that customers who continue to buy from you are loyal. They may simply not have had a better offer — yet.

Stay connected

Do the little things that keep relationships alive. In lieu of love notes to customers, you can reach out via newsletters, emails, direct-mail pieces, telephone calls, letters and surveys.

Offer special promotions

If you want your customers to do something, you have to do something for them. To make customers feel special, advertise an exclusive offer only for your best customers. Promotions can range from coupons and volume discounts to customer-only sales events.

Be choosy

Relationships are a two-way street. Some customers require so much maintenance that you lose money by serving them. Others buy so infrequently that it costs more to stay connected than it's worth. Develop a tracking system that identifies your most profitable customers, and concentrate on keeping these relationships healthy.

STREET SMART ACTION PLAN

- Wow new customers.
- Follow up.
- Get feedback.
- Don't take customers for granted.
- Stay connected.
- Offer special promotions.

Chapter 42

Survey your Customers to Improve Your Business

Part 3 of 4

An online customer feedback survey is a powerful tool that helps you identify areas you can improve or enhance in your business or organization, according to Marc Ankerman, business professor at *The* Ohio State University and former Director of Learning and Development at Express (a division of Limited Inc.) He suggests that there are many advantages of conducting such surveys including:

Getting information you might not know. The only way to know what your customers are thinking about your business is to ask them. The survey provides your customers an opportunity to answer the specific questions and comment on other areas you may not have thought about.

Supporting your goals

Your survey shares with your customers additional information about your services or products. You can also find out if a price increase will be accepted, if your prices are too high, or if it is time to add or delete certain products from your inventory.

Telling your story

The survey indirectly explains the reasons why you do the type of business you are doing.

Setting a Standard Operating Procedure.

When your employees know your expectations the standard operating procedures become second nature to them. They are more likely to perform to those achievable standards. When your customers know the basics of what to expect, you can figure out ways to surprise them with greater service and quality, which assures repeat business.

Ankerman suggests these four steps to effectively conducting your online surveys.

Step One: Meet With Your Staff.

The initial meeting is essential to insure that you and your team are prepared to receive the feedback and design survey questions which relate to the issues (both positive and negative).

Step Two: Identify Areas

You Want To Improve. It is great to get compliments and hear about all the good things you're doing for your customers. However, to improve your business you want to know those items that your customers would like to see enhanced, changed or dropped. Design your questions to generate basic feedback so that your survey provides you with specific details.

Step Three: Tease

At Broadway Bound, a local dance studio, they used a "teaser survey" with kids first. Although they were mainly interested in parental feedback, the kids survey got the parents involved and allowed them to discover important information about both groups. A catch phrase about the survey was created and put up on an electronic bulletin board to let everyone know the surveys were coming: They even created a contest and gave away T-shirts to the kids for turning in their e-mail addresses. Do whatever works to get the message out that the information was important. As time passed, the parents asked when their survey would be coming!

Part Four: Prepare to Act!

Conducting your survey means being prepared to make changes and act on the suggestions. Even if you cannot act on all of the ideas, you must be prepared to consider and respond to the comments and issues raised by a survey. Once you do act, it shows your customer that you care about your business and are ready to make changes for the better.

Smart Marketing Action Plan:

- Ask your staff for their survey ideas.
- Identify possible areas of improvement.
- Use survey teasers to start.
- Act on the information.
- Check out www.zoomerang.com for e-survey ideas.

For info: http://www.case-chosencandidates.com

Chapter 43

Taking Care Of Your Customers Critical to Surviving Slow Times

Customer retention and referral have always been critical to a successful business. But now, more than ever, due to the current tough economic climate, you may want to review your current level of customer satisfaction. Once you review, you'll create a simple plan-of-attack to shore up any weakness. We've conducted numerous seminars and have consulted many clients on this subject. According to our clients, here are two of the most effective techniques:

Conduct Courtesy Telephone Survey

When your foot traffic is down or your inbound inquiries are a fraction of what they were, you and your staff may find you have some free time. Use this time to get on the phone and contact your customers. Tell them that you're conducting a "courtesy survey" and would like to get their input. With their permission, ask them four or five (no more) questions about the service they get from your company. Design the questions so that you get useful information, not merely confirmation of what you want to hear. For example, "If we could change one thing about the service we provided you that would have made it better, what would that be? This question assumes that there is room for improvement. Most people would ask, "was everything okay?" and the standard response is a perfunctory "yes." The first question does a much better job of making it easy for your customers to tell you how, from their perspective, you could make it better for them.

Train and Evaluate Service Quality

Most of your customers first come in contact with your business when they call or visit your business. You can't expect your employees to behave a certain way if you haven't trained them to do so. Once they've had a seminar or another type of training program, it'll reinforce their behavior.

For example, one of our clients had a problem with their front line people forgetting to ask the customer if he or she would like to set up an appointment for the next visit. This simple act increases repeat business dramatically because it doesn't rely on the customer to call in for an appointment. To change the behavior we recommended a simple contest. The owner of the company had several of his friends service as "secret shoppers." If the secret shopper was asked to set up the next appointment, he would hand that employee, on the spot, a $20 bill. On the other had, if he was not asked for the appointment, the employee received a card explaining that he or she just missed out on the $20 spiff.

After the first employee learned of his $20 misfortune, the word started to spread. Then a few won the $20 bill prize. After that nearly every employee asked for the next appointment. This behavior lasted long after the contest ended.

Smart Marketing Action Plan:

- Telephone survey your customers to find out how you can improve.
- Ask questions that make it easy for them to give you useful information.
- Keep the survey short, no more than five questions.

- At the end of the survey, thank them for time and offer to send them a small gift certificate.
- Conduct a brief seminar to teach the behaviors to improve your level customers satisfaction.
- Use the secret shopper contest to reinforce the desired front line behavior.
- Use a specific secret shopper once at any given location.
- Reward success on the spot.
- If the reward is not earned, the employee is given a card explaining why.

Chapter 44

Managing A Difficult Employee

Part 4 of 4

It happens all the time. You make a great hiring decision and then at some point in the process of the employee's tenure, you question your hiring decision. Difficult employees tend to be a difficult and lengthy topic. However, Marc Ankerman, business professor at *The* Ohio State University and former Director of Learning and Development at Express (a division of Limited Inc.) suggests a few things you can do to ease the pain of this situation before it gets out of hand.

Set clear goals

If the goals for the employee are etched in stone, it makes it much easier for the employer to provide feedback about behavior. Let's assume we define our difficult employee as having a number of issues. If the issues deal with the work effort, then clear, descriptive and measurable accomplishments need to be described by the employer. If an employee is not 100 percent certain of what they have to do to meet the objectives, they are often seen as "difficult" This can also include the methods for accomplishing the work. The clearer you can be, the better the communication and chance that there is no misunderstanding of what needs to be accomplished.

Have regular reviews of progress

Once those goals have been set, it is important to keep track of the work which is accomplished. If you normally would have monthly updates with your employees, consider a weekly update with this more challenging employee. Even if the meetings are brief, make the employee document progress and pitfalls of the actions they are taking. If they realize that you are up to speed with the issues, the chances are they will have less time or chance to complain about issues, or make things "difficult." Progress meetings should always have an agenda, which outlines what you are looking for in the update, and a timeline for future explanations and updates.

Identify open discussions of issues

Many companies say they have an open-door policy, and this is great, but make sure you and this employee are communicating. If you hear of issues or concerns, bring them out into the open quickly. When you feel that "difficulties" are imminent, schedule additional time to put the issues to rest, and focus on the outcomes. Make the employee feel that they can bring these items to your attention, while asking the employee to assist in the solution. If they are willing to bring the issues out into the open, you have to adjust to having them be an agent of change and opportunity for solutions as well.

Plan on next steps

Most companies have plans of action and steps, which can be taken to initiate disciplinary actions. If the employee continues to be difficult, it is the responsibility of the supervisor to deal with the situation. Far too often, managers and supervisors ignore the warning signs and hope things will get better. Make plans for action in cases of difficulty with an employee. Give them fair warning of the consequences of the action, and indicate what behavior you expect before your next review of performance. It is the action you take in the process, which will help you in the long run.

SMART MARKETING ACTION PLAN:

- Set clear goals. Make sure you are on a level playing field. Everyone knows what is expected.

- Have regular reviews of progress. Meet often to review accomplishments and expectations.

- Identify open discussions of issues.

- Make sure the lines of communication are free and issues can be discussed.

- Don't wait. Be assertive in planning your action.

For info: http://www.case-chosencandidates.com

Chapter 45

Using Good Parenting Skills to Improve Management Skills

You can use effective parenting skills to improve your business success, according to Dr. Norman Shub of the Gestalt Institute. After attending one of his parenting seminars, it became very clear that his ideas, approaches and techniques would be just as appropriate for business people as they are for parents. Of course, this is not to suggest that you should treat your employees or bosses like children. Rather, you should use the same clear communication techniques whether you're raising a family or building your business. Dr. Shub, who also runs Business of People, told us that he does, in fact, teach similar techniques to business people. Here are some of his ideas:

Connection

Nothing happens without connecting to the person with whom you're communicating. Before you can have meaningful communication, you must first engage the other person. This means when someone first approaches, you should give them your undivided attention for the first several minutes. For example, after being away from your home or office, spend the first few minutes connecting with those who need it. Chances are they will feel that connection and then let you get back to your other tasks. If, on the other hand you put that person off, they will continue to pester you. Many managers, as well as parents, have years of knowledge that they wish to impart. Dr. Shub warns that the first job of a parent or a manger is not to educate, but connect.

Melting

Melting is the ability to deal with difficult situations effectively, without defending yourself. When you're involved in a heated argument, it is the absolute worst time to deal with issues, or even worse yet, give a lecture. Rather, you must manage the other person's distress, stay open and not rigid. Wait until things settle down before you start addressing issues. If not, the behavior becomes the issue and you don't provide yourself an opportunity to address the vital elements that affect your business.

Manage Conflict

To be effective you need to separate the anger from the conflict. Conflict is a normal part of business, but you can't deal with real problems if the other person is angry. Once you distill anger from the situation, whether it's your anger or the other person's, you'll then be able to better address the specifics that are keeping you from reaching a solution or agreement.

Answering vs. Responding

"Answering" is telling the other person what you think about what they said. Whereas, "responding" is understanding what is said. You do this by asking thoughtful questions, listening, and avoiding giving advice at that time. All too often, when people are upset, the boss tells them what their "problem" is. This makes it worse. Good managers help their people work through those difficult issues.

Support

This is perhaps the most difficult of all. Support is allowing the other person to learn from their mistakes. You don't want to rush in and alleviate their struggle. The struggle is critical to the learning process. If you are always fixing things for your people, they become codependent on you. Allow them to fail.

STREET FIGHTER ACTION PLAN:

- Engage the other person first.
- Don't educate, connect.
- Manage the anger by melting.
- Separate the anger from the conflict.
- Learn to respond, not to answer.
- Be supportive by allowing your people to learn from failure.

Chapter 46

Getting the Sale of a Lifetime

Closing the sale of a lifetime requires a special attitude, according to Rich Gladin; a Houston based sales rep that recently bagged a $2 million sale. Gladin is a Houston based defibrillator sales rep for ZOLL Medical Corporation. After two years and surviving the sales equivalent of a "code blue," he resuscitated the sales effort, which turned out to be the largest ever in his industry. Gladin shared with us some of the key principles he feels allowed him to close this seemingly impossible deal.

Integrity

Prior to working for ZOLL, Gladin worked for two other medial companies for the previous 12 years. He always did his best to satisfy his customer's needs. Then when he started with ZOLL, he had a stellar reputation for making good on his promises. So, when he called on a key decision maker at the hospital about this new biphasic waveform technology developed by ZOLL, he was well received.

Tenacity

It takes a patience and perseverance to sell high-ticket items that have a longer buying cycle. Staying the course was critical to his ultimate success of his effort.

Strategic Preparation

In a sense, success was preordained due to the vision by ZOLL management. The first decision was the development and patenting of a new waveform, a type of technology that allowed ZOLL's biphasic defibrillator to perform significantly better than the two major competitor's technology. This was a "product" decision. The next was a "marketing" decision. ZOLL commissioned various independent research projects that provided conclusive scientific proof that their device did, in fact, perform better for the patients than the competitors. The competition had little, if any such research to support their claims.

Tactical Preparation, Flexibility and Adaptability

When Gladin and his team make their presentation to the committee, they had a technical glitch. The projection system didn't work. Having presentation equipment difficulties when pitching a product can totally turn off the buyers. Fortunately, the team was so well prepared and so passionate about their product, that they were still able to make a powerful presentation.

Universal Support.

Though Gladin was the point person on the project, he had a team of specialists out of the corporate office, including the President of the company, willing to fly to Houston and help in dealing with all aspects of the sale.

Suggest Add-Ons

One interesting development (after they made their presentation) was an invitation to rebid, adding three additional perimeters. Think of this as adding profitable options to a basic unit. This could be looked at as the medical device equivalent of adding power windows, power seats, and a GPS that makes the basic machine more useful. These add-ons to the 180 basic units brought the original proposal of $1.2 million to $2 million.

Success Breeds Success

The postscript to this example is that Gladin was talking to another large hospital that competes directly with the one that just bought the new defibrillators. His contact tells him, "Well if they have them . . . then we have to have them too." This also looks like a sale in the $2 million range.

SMART MARKETING ACTION PLAN:

- Always maintain your integrity.
- Never give up.
- Get support every where you can.
- Prepare for every contingency.
- Invest in ways to prove your claims.
- Use your success to repeat your success.

Chapter 47

How to Negotiate Higher Prices

You don't have to be a victim of predatory price hunting during price negotiations, according to Tom Reilly, a professional speaker and author of *Value Added Selling*. A purchasing agent at Boeing once said, "If salespeople only understood how powerful they are, they could close us down tomorrow."

If that is true that "knowledge is power," then what you don't know holds great power over you. Mr. Reilly believes that knowledge is empowerment. The more you know, the more empowered you feel. Your knowledge of simple negotiating principles will boost your confidence and your competence. Here are six of Mr. Reilly's principles for negotiating a higher price:

Principle One: Your attitude

If you begin the negotiation with the attitude that it must result in a win-win outcome, all the games, gambits, and maneuvers people use, are unnecessary. Your guiding principle must be that, if it's not a good deal for one of you, it's not a good deal for either of you.

Principle Two: Use time to your advantage

Buyers know that if they can get you to make a quick and emotional decision on pricing issues it will probably benefit them more than it will benefit you. More concessions are made at the end of a negotiation, once the momentum is established. Professional negotiators will hold their most important request for that moment when the other person sees light at the end of the tunnel, because they know that more concessions are made at the end of a negotiation.

Principle Three: See the game

Any game you recognize as a game or gambit has less power over you. If you are dealing with a customer who has a predictable, first-response outrage to any price increase, you can prepare yourself for the emotional barrage. If you're dealing with someone who always leads with unreasonable demands, knowing this, makes it easier for you to separate the background noise from the conversation.

Principle Four: Balk at the first offer

Negotiators call this "flinching." This is another way of saying, "Be patient." Do not jump too quickly when the other person makes an offer. It may not be their final offer; it could be an opening move to test the water. Again, use time to your advantage. There may be flexibility in the buyer's negotiating position, but if you are too quick to accept their initial offer, you may not discover areas of flexibility.

Principle Five: Don't split first

Whoever first offers to split the difference will go more than fifty percent of the way. This applies to time as well as money. If you are $2,000 apart from your buyer's budget and you offer to meet the buyer half way, you will likely hear: "That's a generous offer, but we're still $1,000 higher than my budget. I need you to sharpen your pencil even more if we're going to do some business." When there is a difference between your price and the price that the buyer wants to pay,

121

ask that person for a suggestion to resolve the issue. The buyer may offer the first split.

Principle Six: Know your walking point

Unless you know your walking point, you could find yourself making concessions you may later regret, once you've had the chance to reflect on the terms of the negotiation. Knowing your walking point builds your confidence and communicates to the buyer that there is a point beyond which you will not go. For information about Tom Reilly's Training log on to www.tomreillytraining.com.

Chapter 48

Hiring Administrative Talent

Without "Breaking the Bank"

(Part 1 of 2)

Even in a tight economy, we all still need to attract and hire great, talented employees — especially good administrative people. Office managers, secretaries and clerks are the human fuel that keeps our businesses running.

I know I would be in deep trouble without my assistant. And, if it was as easy as just running an ad in the Sunday paper, we would all have perfect administrative people working for us. But even with a plentiful labor pool, it is still difficult to find just the right people to fit in and help us move our business forward.

In these next two chapters, I will share with you a simple four-step process that removes the doubt, uncertainty and guesswork form your hiring. And, it will save you time, money and the headaches of managing hiring mistakes.

Know What You Are Looking For

Step one is to build a profile of the successful person. Too often, we go into the hiring process with only a vague idea of what we really want. A good profile includes two parts. First you have to identify "what the person must accomplish to be successful", and second you have to identify "what the person needs to know, be able to do and how they go about it" to be successful.

Start by putting down in writing (yes I said in writing) a list of all the things this person needs to accomplish to be successful. This is not a list of responsibilities. It is a list of the things you need this person to accomplish. A good way to get this done is to list your outcomes according to time frames, short, medium and long term. For example, if you are hiring a secretary, your list might look like this:

1. Design and implement a new filing system.

2. Generated basic correspondence and reports accurately.

3. Put system in place to manage ordering and maintaining inventory of supplies.

4. Delivered process improvement for existing systems.

5. Accurately manage the Manager's calendar.

You notice that these are not a list of responsibilities. Instead, they are specific outcomes that will help you run your business. This list represents the first step in hiring great administrative talent.

The second step of the profile is to simply translate your outcomes into a list of knowledge skills and abilities. The easiest way to do this is to answer the following three questions.

1. What does the person need to know to be successful?

2. What does the person need to be able to do to be successful?

3. How does the person need to behave to be successful?

These questions will help you identify the requirements for success on the job.

Chapter 49

Recruit Faster and For Less Money

(Part 2 of 2)

Step two is to identify and recruit a good pool of candidates to choose from. You start by developing a strategy. A few minutes of preparation will save you time and money down the road.

Begin by answering one simple question, "Why should someone work for you?" This may seem simple, but the answer will help you choose the right strategy for attracting candidates and make your recruiting more focused. I call this your Unique Hiring Proposition (UHP). Some possible answers include: We pay well, We offer good benefits, We offer options for advancement, We work with the latest equipment.

Once you know why a person should work for you, your next step is to determine where to look for them. The first and best place to look is for referrals from your existing employees. Ask them who they know. A referral from an existing employee is always your first, best choice.

Here is a simple rule to follow when you have to look outside your company for candidates: Work Backwards! Try to think about where the candidates are today. If they are working, where are they working?

What do they read? Where do they congregate? What websites or blogs do they frequent? When you can determine where they are now, you can design the right strategy to reach them.

If they are unemployed, you reach them through on-line job sites, in the classified ads and through your state unemployment department. If they congregate at a health club, it might be as simple as posting a 3x5 card on a bulletin board. Always look for the simple easy solution before you try the traditional or difficult option.

Finally, use your UHP when you do advertise. Don't put up a 3x5 card that says "Secretary" Instead, try a headline that matches your UHP like "Come Join the Fastest Growing CPA Firm in Cleveland" This gives them a reason to be interested which happens to be consistent with your company.

A few simple, inexpensive techniques should help you build a targeted candidate pool.

Picking the Best

Now that you have generated a group of candidates to choose from, you need to use a system to pick the best. This is step three in the process. I use a simple philosophy when it comes to choosing people. "The more data you get, the better decision you make" So your challenge is to get as much information as you can, using as many sources as possible. Your steps may include as many of the following as possible:

- Phone screen
- Phone interview
- Skype interview
- In-person interview
- Multiple interviews
- Testing
- Reference checks

Start with a simple phone screen. Ten minutes on the phone should give you enough information to determine if you should to invest more time with the person. Try to get some information about the person's phone skills and one other requirement. Four or five questions should do the trick.

Sometimes a phone screen will turn into a full-blown interview by phone. Take as much time as you need to make up your mind about bringing the person in for a face to face interview.

Next comes the face to face interview. The key to the success of the interview is the quality of questions you ask the person. The better your questions, the better information you get.

There are four types of questions you should ask in an interview.

Factual Questions: Ask questions that require the person to give you factual information. What word processing software did you use? How often did you interface with clients?

Action Questions: These questions get the person to tell you what they have done. How did you implement the new filing system? How did you solve the customer's problem?

Probing Questions: You need to ask questions to get specifics. Think of you first question as the tip of the iceberg. Who else was involved? How long did it take you? What else did you try?

Examples: Get examples of things they have done that are the same or similar to the things you need them to do on your job. How did you implement the new filing system? What specific types of correspondence did you prepare for your manager?

Prepare your questions in advance. And, make certain you ask questions about each of the requirements you identified in your profile. A simple way to organize your questions and your interview is to simply walk the person through their career. Start at the beginning, the person's first job, and work toward the present. Ask questions about each requirement at each job in the person's background.

Another option in your data gathering process is testing. There are two types of testing, skills and personality. I am in favor of any technique that adds more data and testing certainly does. A great site for more information on testing is www.effectiveselection.com.

Make Your Decision Easy

The final step is to make the decision. The decision is the easiest part if you have done a good job of the previous three steps. All you need to do is match the data you gathered against the profile you built in the beginning. For each requirement, see if the person has demonstrated the knowledge skill and ability to be successful.

With the changing market conditions, the burden has switched form finding good candidates for jobs to picking the best of the available pool. By using this simple four-step process, you will give yourself the best chance of hiring great administrative talent.

For more information on the Selecting Winners process and to order, *How To Hire The Dream Employee Every Time,* send an e-mail to freebook@selectingwinners.com or fax the same information to 206-230-6487.

Chapter 50

Relieving Financial Stress

Angie Hollerich is a Columbus-based certified educational planner, professional speaker and author. Her book, is *Tips from the Top: Targeted Advice from America's Top Money Minds.* Previously an investment advisor and financial planner, she focuses on managing weight and wealth. She offers a few steps to relieving financial stress:

Implementing a budget based on income expenses is the most important foundation for both personal and business finance. Obviously, you need to know how much money is coming in to estimate monthly, quarterly and annual projections. A lot of times business owners just shoot from the hip and don't do business projections — in fact, 80 percent of businesses don't even have a written plan.

When realizing your budget, understand that your business may be seasonal, or times may be inherently slow and prepare for such occurrences. "When you prepare for the feast, you need to prepare for the famine," Hollerich says. In such a situation, you should always have money available to you without consequence and have your budget prioritized by what line items must be paid. For example, employees and taxes must always take priority and be paid on time, while other items may be credited until more prosperous times.

Understanding how you deal with finances personally has a huge implication on your financial success as a businessperson. If you have poor personal financial habits or strategies, they will spill over into your business life. Observe how you manage your own money. Pay attention to whether or not you procrastinate and how stringently you keep records — these will all impact how you handle your company finances.

When you own a business, there are many things you would like to have right away. But when it comes to developing a business strategy, you should focus on what you need right away. According to Hollerich, "We in America want instant gratification, we have to sometimes deny ourselves the things we want but don't necessarily need; we have to sacrifice some of the bells and whistles." Instead of purchasing something with cash, people tend to charge it. Or, they tend to supply themselves with more inventory than necessary, wasting cash for the business.

Involving interested parties in financial planning helps those who spend your money get aligned with your goals. Outline your financial strategies personally to your family members and professionally to your employees. Make employees fiscally responsible for their department and have an accountability employee expense report to keep a handle on everyone's ability to meet their budget. If you over fund or under fund one department, inform the employees and readjust your budget accordingly.

Always explore saving and investment opportunities. Include such a plan in your budget to fall under your line items instead of eating away at your discretionary savings. The reason you get into business is to eventually start making money. To provide for your long-term goals, you are likely to put in 60 to 80 hour per week. But, a smart investment plan could ensure that you won't have to work in the long run.

The most crucial blow to your entire financial situation is procrastination. We tend not to do things that are hard, or at least things that are perceived to be difficult. Planning and executing a budget, writing a business plan, educating yourself — these are vital components that many businesses overlook and pay the price for not making the effort to do it right the first time. Procrastinating your financial responsibility only makes achieving success more expensive, time-consuming and stressful.

SMART MARKETING ACTION PLAN:

- Plan and execute a strong budget.
- Be prepared for sluggish times by prioritizing your expenses.

- Develop good money habits personally to be realized professionally.
- Get your employees involved.
- Explore opportunities for saving and investment.
- Act now — Don't procrastinate!

Chapter 51

The Power of Twenty

You can get a lot more done in your day by following some simple steps, according to Cindy Kubica, of Studio 10 in Nashville, Tennessee. A communications expert and trainer, Kubica advises her clients that they can get totally organized by using her "rule of twenty," which represents using only twenty minutes a day. Your first step is to update your To-Do list. Transfer all incomplete items from past lists. She warns that as you review your list you begin to feel frustrated because too many items have been carried over from list to list to list. Don't panic. The solution to your problem is only twenty minutes away. The first of five steps will be the hardest, but you can do it. Here's how you get started:

Step One. Tell your coworkers, children, or your spouse that you are 'taking twenty' and please do not disturb. Be firm. Don't take calls during this 20 minute period, which is a great use for voice mail. Close the door to your office. Put up a "do not disturb" sign" if necessary. Most interruptions can wait 20 minutes. Others will respect your time if you respect your time.

Step Two. Set a timer for 20 minutes.

Step Three. Grab a small stack of papers you've been meaning to file, or empty one drawer you've wanted to clean out.

Step Four. File, sort, or organize until all items are put in their proper place. Look for every excuse to throw things out. Rule of thumb:

"When it doubt, toss it out."

Step Five. (This step is the next hardest step.).When the timer goes off - STOP! You work for twenty minutes only, (no matter were you are in the task). Tomorrow, pick up where you left off. If you continue to work, you will end up in the same place with your list getting longer and longer.

This system works, if you work it. If you're serious about getting organized, Kubica urges you to use this system exactly as she as presented it. No deviations, especially with the "minute" rule. Get in the habit of starting each day with the "power of twenty." Starting your day with an accomplishment makes you feel good and takes a little of the sting out of the times when you feel pulled in ten different directions and can't get anything done.

You will discover in no time at all that you can delete a pile of papers from your desk, unpack a box that has been sitting around for months, or clean out your dresser—one drawer at a time. Complete small fragments of a large task and you'll replace that overwhelmed feeling with a wonderful sense of achievement. You will be amazed at how much you can accomplish —just twenty minutes at a time.

SMART MARKETING ACTION PLAN:

- Compile your list of things to do.
- Set a timer for 20 minutes.
- Choose a pile.
- File and toss.
- When the alarm goes off, stop!
- Repeat daily.
- Develop requirements to identify weakness.

Chapter 52

Discovering Your Company's Personality

Just as every company is differentiated by what it produces, every company has different values and characteristics that determine its unique personality. Authors Sandra Feteke and LeeAnna Keith, in their book *Companies are People Too*, share a test to help you determine the personality of your company. By identifying the personality of your organization, you can raise your company's performance. Feteke and Keith provide a test they call the "CAP2" (which stands for Companies Are People Too). This simple test is composed of 84 questions and is taken by your company's leaders to determine your values, character, and strengths. Though neither expensive nor time consuming, the CAP2 test helps you put your organization's personality type to work for you to make better decisions. Think of this test as an "entrepreneurial X-Ray." However once you've identified those areas that need fixing, you must then be open to actually fixing them.

The test is broken down into four components. Your company or organization's personality is determined by which dimension of the four decision making components they relate to:

Focusing Energy

How your company focuses its energy depends on whether you are extroverted or introverted. Extroverted companies focus on markets, competitors, partners, or various corporate sponsors. They learn by doing and usually have a strong public relations department. Introverted companies tend to focus on technology, values, and opportunities to grow. They research before taking actions, and focus mainly on technology and specialized consumer markets.

Gathering Information

Gathering information influences behavior. "Sensing" organizations, for example, incorporate the five physical senses. This type of organization listens to the customer, and observes details. Contrast that to the "Intuitive" organization which focuses on the big picture using market data. They seek out new, challenging ways of doing things, and are willing to take risks.

Making Decisions

Decision making preferences influence how an organization understands and acts based on information. An organization that relies on thinking, guides itself by logic. They adhere to the rules. On the other end are "Feeling" organizations who are guided by values. Their goal is harmony and do not like criticism. The rules can be bent.

Structuring Work

The way your company structures its work determines the way it relates to the world. The structure of work is determined by factors such as responsiveness to change, procedure, and scheduling. For example, "Judging" organizations base their strategies and decisions on predictability. They favor strict schedules, planning, and focus on following through. Where as "Perceiving" companies tend toward flexibility in their environment, individual initiative, and pay close attention to market conditions.

Once you discover your company's personality, use this information to strive for a higher level of performance and promote long term prosperity. You will become consistent, and attract more customers by discovering how to get critical tasks done. When you look at your CAP2 profile, you can see what you have in common with larger, well known companies.

STREET FIGHTER ACTION PLAN:

- Have your company leaders take the CAP2 test.
- Determine which dimension of each of the four components of decision making your company holds.
- After determining your company's strengths, weaknesses, and goals, find its personality.
- Make a list of five tasks that will help your company reach a higher performance level.
- Choose one action step and implement it.
- Repeat the last step for all other steps.

Sneak Preview of
Smart Selling

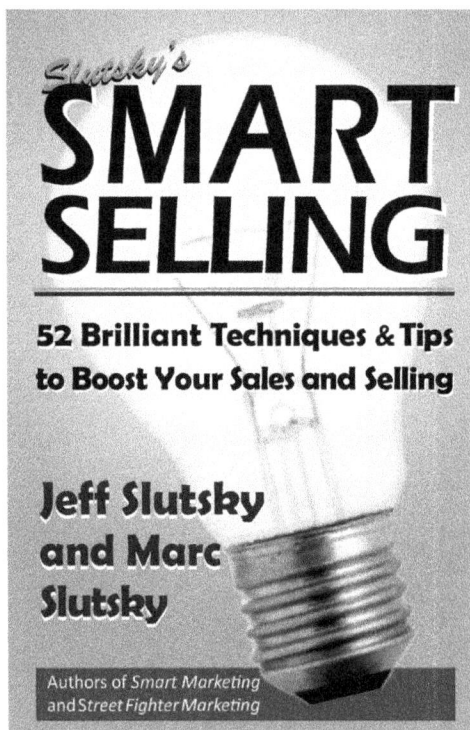

Order your copy online today at:
www.createspace.com/4411673

Chapter 1

Think of Selling Like You Would Dating

Nearly everybody in your organization sells, not just your sales people. You may have to sell a product or service or even and idea. Yet, selling basics are sometimes difficult to grasp. To help understand selling basics, think of selling as if you're dating. According to Pamela Lanier, President of It's Just Lunch, a Columbus dating service, "Most people share too much information about themselves on a first date." The same thing happens on many first time sales calls.

Prospecting

Like dating, selling first depends on making the initial call. Fear of rejection often keeps us from getting on the phone and asking for that first visit. But, if you don't make the call, you'll never get the date.

Pre-Date

Present your best side. Dress appropriately and if in doubt, error on the upscale side. Be on your best behavior. Mind your manners. You are being judged the entire time. If the first encounter is a lunch, choose a place that's quiet enough to have a conversation and has good service.

Qualifying

The first date, like the first sales call is for qualifying your prospect. There is where most people make their mistake, both in dating and selling. You need to determine if this person meets the key criteria needed to establish a potential relationship. After all, in both situations, you're not looking for a one-night stand.

Probing

Once you qualify your prospect, dig deeper to find out your prospect's needs and wants. Do this before you start sharing too much information about you (or your company and product). If you sense that this prospect is going to be high maintenance, probe some more to see if the ultimate value justifies the extra attention. Don't interrupt when the other person is talking. You need to interpret what they say with what they really mean.

Objections

As in any sale, there are bound to be objections. You must determine just how critical each objection is. You also need to determine if the objection is legitimate or if your prospect is looking for an excuse to get rid of you. If there is no way to overcome the objection, you may be forced to re-evaluate the potential of the relationship.

Closing The Sale

After an appropriate number of sales calls (or dates) it's time to get their commitment. If all the other steps were handled properly, this should be the easiest part of the process. Sales, like dating, should be a win-win.

Service After The Sale

After the client commits, then it's up to you to make the relationship work. This is often where the hard work comes into play. Just because you have a contract doesn't mean you have to stop working.

take it for granted . . . or you may find that your life long customer gets buyers' remorse and starts seeking proposals from your competition.

SMART SELLING ACTION PLAN:

- Think of selling like dating.
- Court your prospect.
- Listen intently and ask probing questions.
- Discover likes, dislikes, needs and wants.
- Once you close the sale, continue with good service.

Chapter 2

Doing Business On The Golf Course

Business is often conducted around the game of golf. Whether you're wooing new clients or working your way up the corporate ladder, your behavior and attitude on the golf course can either help or hinder your success. Here are some tips from successful business people who golf for fun and business.

Sig Munster (handicap:10) a Senior Vice President of Morgan Stanley in Columbus, Ohio plays golf with business prospects to size up a person's character, and to see if he wants to do business with this person. There are many behaviors that would cause alarm including: cheating on the score; rudeness to the caddy; not raking the sand traps, throwing clubs, miss marking the ball, etc. Munster guesses that 25 - 30 percent of his business can be attributed to his time on the golf course. "It's a great way to build long term relationships, some which have lasted over 40 years. It gives you something in common with someone." It doesn't matter how good a player you are, according to Munster. It's literally how you play the game that counts when it comes to business. He also feels that membership in a prestigious golf course is also important because it makes it easier for you to attract players, especially top level decision makers.

Steve Miller, (handicap:1.6) President of The Adventure, a Seattle based trade show consulting firm, generally doesn't bring up business on the course unless the client does. He suggests that if you want to bring up business, don't do it too early in the round and don't try to do too much business. Golf is a social event. So being too intense about business can ruin the overall enjoyment of the round. Miller suggests that you should keep current with the PGA Golf Tour, so you can carry on a conversation other than business.

Mark Mayfield, (handicap: 4) a Kansas City based professional speaker, advises letting your guest set the pace with respects to wagering, alcohol and style of play. You'll know after the first green if that person is a stickler with the rules or prefers mulligans and give-me putts. Keep it light. Don't do heavy duty selling on the course, but rather use the time to gather some information and only share a few general points at the most. Mayfield feels that if you give so much information that the client has to take notes and bring their smart phone, you'll probably turn them off. Mayfield shared a story of a very competitive golfer who bet a prospective client $50 a hole. He won the bet but lost the deal.

John McCoy, former Chairman of Bank One. (handicap: no comment).

SMART SELLING ACTION PLAN:

- Be on your best behavior. Your character is being evaluated on the golf course. Cheating, temper tantrums, rudeness and other unsportsmanlike conduct will cost you business.

- Join prestigious golf clubs. The higher level of prestige you can afford, the easier it is to attract players, especially higher level decision makers.

- Don't talk business unless your client brings it up. Use the game as a way to build the relationship. Limit the business talk to before or after the round.

- Let the client set the pace. Follow the client's lead with regards to alcohol, betting and style of play. Keep current with events on the PGA tour. It gives you something to talk about.

Street Fighter Audio & Video Program

5 Videos (MP4),
15 audios (MP3) and
3 Workbooks (PDF)
on <u>one flash drive</u>.

Only $399.00.

Call 800-758-8759.

Index

www.ingramcontent.com/pod-product-compliance
Lightning Source LLC
Chambersburg PA
CBHW071855200326
41519CB00016B/4400